Easy
Walking

Easy Walking

Walking

Jonathan Lewis Nasaw

J. B. Lippincott Company
Philadelphia & New York

This story is true, whatever that means. The names
of the characters and places have been changed to
protect the privacy of those involved.

U.S. Library of Congress Cataloging in Publication Data

Nasaw, Jonathan Lewis, birth date
    Easy walking.

    Autobiographical.
    1. Paralysis—Personal narratives.   2.   Paraplegics—
Rehabilitation.   3.   Nasaw, Jonathan Lewis, birth date
I.   Title.
RD796.N37A33   362.4'3'0924 [B]   74-23446
ISBN—0-397-01078-8

dedicated to sparrow and the family stone

Think no more, lad; laugh, be jolly:
    Why should men make haste to die?
Empty heads and tongues a-talking
Make the rough road easy walking,
And the feather pate of folly
    Bears the falling sky.

from *A Shropshire Lad*
by A. E. Housman

Easy Walking

1

Don't Fade Away

I've had a dream of a dark country road, street lamps on telephone poles making round yellow circles in the darkness—good night Mrs. Calabash—and I am in the car sliding slowly along the seat as the car rolls over and over while I laugh and laugh.

But now I'm awake, and around me the semidarkness is spotlit by random pools of light, ghost-light of monitors glowing white and winking red and cardiac tracers popping and flowing white lines on green screens.

There are white figures floating through the room, it seems—one glides toward me. I shut my eyes for fear of a spirit, and open them to see a pleasant-faced young man with horn-rimmed glasses standing over me with a clipboard. He speaks:

"Cough."

I do.

And as the resultant pain accompanies me to unconsciousness I remind myself to mark the guy down as a real prick.

When I awaken again it is in daylight, and although I am obviously in a hospital I ask, "Where am I?"

A slack-jawed old black man who is pushing a broom answers me, "Icy Ewe."

"Hunh?"

"I . . . C . . . U . . ."

"I see you too," I answer, and it seems so funny that I laugh, but my laugh rings with hysteria and echoes down a black corridor in my mind. Then a nurse hurries to my bed, raises a syringe to the light, and as she jabs me, that dark corridor melts in a rich golden glow, and I fade, fade away.

That's All Right, Roy, I'm Only Bleeding

"I'm fine, Ma. Really. I got it made in da shade," is what I tell one of the faces that floats now and again above my bed. Those faces, they all look so damned worried, take my mother for instance, her eyes always get red when she cries, so she wears sunglasses, so when she wears sunglasses you know she's been crying. She's wearing sunglasses now.

And she doesn't understand that everything's all right. Really. It's nice and peaceful, and before anything can hurt, a pretty nurse will give me a shot. So everything's fine. Except.

Except for my bed. It makes me think of Roy Campanella. I can't stop thinking about Roy Campanella.

I picture him closing up his liquor store one night, totaling the register, shutting the lights, locking the door, and I picture him behind the wheel, see him skidding in the rainy dark, picture him pinned in the overturned wreckage of his goddam big American car, unable to move, unable even to shut off the ignition, waiting for an explosion that never comes.

One more picture. I see him waking up in a hospital strapped into some sort of a steel and canvas frame. So when I awaken and look around me, find myself in a hospital room, with no memory of having gotten there, find myself face down on a canvas-stretcher-in-a-steel-frame contraption, I scarcely have to ask any questions, even when they clap another stretcher on my back, clamp it down, and spin me around to face the ceiling without my having moved a muscle or changed the relative position of my body an iota.

I am, I know, in a Stryker frame with a broken back, and little Willie Nasaw's childhood reading of the autobiographies of Roy Campanella and a half-dozen other inspirational cripples has not been in vain.

Letters from Hazel

Day, night, what the fuck? Night now, and strange things are happening in Intensive Care. I lie quietly, my tubes (one in, one out) clear and flowing. I am easing off on a hundred milligrams of Demerol and a grain and a half of Seconal.

In the next bed (there are a dozen here in ICU, scattered seemingly at random) Hazel lies curled, bones hollow like a bird's. Different strokes for different folks. Hazel had a whopper, and she lies on her side, weightless as a doll, but all day her eyes are flopped open and staring. She's my nearest neighbor, but our communications have been somewhat limited.

"Aphasia," said a nurse. "Like a crossed wire from

13

her brain to her mouth. She knows what she wants to say, but the words come out different. Say she wants a glass of water, she might ask for a fountain pen. Isn't that funny?"

Yeah. Sometimes. Like this afternoon. Her whole damn family was in for a visit, one at a time. Her husband came first, wearing his second-best suit, the one he sleeps in.

"How have you been?" he asked.

"No T," she said.

"No, no tea, you don't have to have any tea," he answered.

"We don't even give her any tea," said the nurse.

"No T. No T, No RST, No P No L No L Noel Noel."

I know, of course, that Hazel's been doing letters for two days. Letters to the morning nurse, letters to the priest, letters to her two old lady schoolteacher friends who visited her yesterday. I know why, too. Her daughter.

Her daughter. Comes in every day. This afternoon she wore a crisp blouse, short soft clinging skirt, her ass glided beneath it, practically in reach of my right arm, which, fuck the luck, is strapped to an armboard, an IV sunk in my hand. So I just watched while the daughter leaned on Hazel.

"Hello, Mom," she said reassuringly. "It's Sis. Ess Eye Ess. Joey's outside. Jay Oh Ee Why. How are you?"

The daughter is a speech therapist.

Hazel flapped her head the other way. She don't wanna *know* about it. I see her point—she lies in the shadowland between the dead and the living, paralyzed, her every need a speechless nightmare, and Sis is starting in on aphasic therapy. The never-too-soon school.

"C'mon, Mom, you can do it." Hazel's hands fluttered, her head flopped from side to side, she gurgled in her throat.

"Well, you better get some rest now, Mom. Are Ee Ess Tea. Because we're going to do lots of work tomorrow. We're going to get you talking again just like new. Bye. Bee Why Ee."

Before that door had even closed completely behind that bee-ootiful behind, Hazel's whole body was jumping in spasms, and her hands were typing feverishly on the nurse's arm.

"No RST," she said. "No R. No S. No T . . ." I don't think she was much up for more work. Maybe she just wanted to die quietly, but anyway, she went on for an hour (Hazel gets no tranqs, nothing for pain. Funny, she never even asks for anything) and I was struck with admiration for her perversity.

That was this afternoon. Tonight, as I say, something strange is going on. I was asleep. I am now awake, for sure, the Seconal finished with its run through my bloodstream, the Demerol fading away, my head almost clear.

For a long time now dope has covered my brain like heavy snow covers the ground. At intervals, pain prods through like a stick from above, and fear comes with the consciousness, poking up like a crocus. Well, every time that crocus pops its goddam head up, I ring my call button and dump two feet of snow on the motherfucker.

But before I can ring tonight, I notice the darkness. Dark, all dark, no sensors, no pulsing lights. Of course. My curtains are drawn. Drawn? From the next bed chirps a high bird voice, Hazel's voice, I recognize it. But no letters. No "No RST." Hazel's voice, piping clear and unrusted, somewhat slurred from stroke.

"Cut it out, you two. Now cut it out. Hey you two. I said cut it out, now. Cut. It. Out."

I hit my buzzer. A nurse's head peeks in between the curtains.

"She's talking," I say. "Hazel's talking. What's going on over there?"

"Aphasia. Doesn't know what she's saying."

But . . .

I think this over for the moment's wait before the nurse brings me my Demerol, and then fade off to the sound of two nurses rustling around the bed next to me while this thin voice warns and pleads and threatens.

"Cut it out, you two. Just cut it out."

I dream that they opened the curtains and Hazel turned to me, spoke, said, "Forgive them, Willie, they know not what they do."

"Bullshit," I said.

They Put a Hurt on Me

It might have been the next day—it might have been the next week for all I knew—I lay watching the medications nurse.

Hazel was quiet—she spoke no more. Not even letters. Her daughter was somewhat exercised at her, but I was proud of her, and told her so when we were alone.

Ah Christ, the Medications Nurse. Her name was Chalice and she was a sweet loving cup. With sweet dark brown hair that she would let down when she worked the last shift, and dark brown eyes that maybe were transplanted from some rose in Spanish Harlem.

I fell in love with her one day as she was stabbing casually through my flesh in search of an elusive vein in which to restart an IV. I fell in love with her because she was beautiful and because, as she hacked and I moaned, she let fall a tear.

Shit. I'll love anybody who cries for me.

This afternoon her hair was up, and she prepared the medications like a priest serving Mass. She read the orders from the charts with a finger gracefully skating along the lines and her lips moving thoughtfully. She raised the hypodermics to the light as she filled them. Clear fluids sparkled and bubbles rose in bottles, fish to the sunlight. Pills she placed in fluted paper cups, and colored liquids, rose and white and ruby, she poured into tiny plastic cups cute as kittens.

Something there is about a nurse's uniform. I have a friend—they call him the captain—Capt Rico (where the hell is Rico? Last time I saw him, he was behind the wheel of this car that was turning over and over). The Capt, at the age of nine, was stricken by infantile paralysis. He was in and out of hospitals until he was just past twelve, but his only scars were psychological. His surroundings, it seems, failed to delay the onset of puberty. They did, however, affect it to the extent that he, for the next twenty years, refused to perform cunnilingus on any female except a nurse in uniform. With standards that high, of course, he did damn little eating out, but when he did, finally, get his wish, it was, he said, well worth the wait. I never shared his phobia, but now, watching Chalice, I could dig his point.

My random lecherous thoughts, though, were idle wanderings—I felt no stirrings below. My drug haze was comfortable, broken in like an old fielder's glove. I watched Chalice with passive faith. I was secure, I was taken care of. Then, through the door of ICU burst a beefy man in crisp white uniform, with a shoulder patch that said "P.T." He walked over to my nurse, put a heavy hand lightly on the small of her back.

"Chalice," he said, "ROM on J. Nasaw. Do you have him?"

"His nickname is Willie," she answered him softly, and pointed at me. I looked back at her, but she didn't meet my eyes. Knowing her feelings about pain (most unprofessional she was, that way) I should have figured something was up, but so drug-dulled was my early warning system that I suspected nothing.

"Willie," he said at my bedside, "my name's George. Your doctor has ordered a little therapy for you, to sort of keep you loose until you're a little stronger."

"Okay," I told him, returning his handshake with a left-hand squeeze. In my warm loving haze, I was even beginning to like the guy a little. He lifted my leg gently, holding it like a rifle in his hands.

"Have you noticed how stiff your legs are?" He held the leg in one hand, supporting it from underneath, just above the knee. The leg did not bend from its own weight, but stayed out stiff. "Just relax it," he said, but I might as well have tried to relax *his* leg, for all the control I had.

"All right," he said, and with his other hand on top of my ankle pushed down hard, strong, slow, and steady.

I disappeared, and returned a millisecond later to the metallic echoes of my own scream. He was forcing the rigid leg to bend, an inch, two inches. I tried to scream for him to stop, but it came out unintelligible in a spray of snot, spit, and tears. He stopped anyway, and no-pain came flooding in to warm me.

"I'm sorry," he said. I opened my eyes, and saw his red face over me, his eyes surprisingly sad. No-pain made me feel a sort of love for him, and I scarcely noticed that he had lifted the other leg into the same position, ready, aim . . .

When the pain hit, I dissolved, I blubbered, from eyes nose mouth I slobbered my face, I whimpered until hiccups took my breath. I noticed only dully when the actual pain began, ended, began, but I know I cried until after he had gone, until Chalice was at my side, gentle hands at my face, gentle needle at my arm. Calm crept into me, and I looked up at her, trying to speak between lessening sobs and hiccups.

"He won't be back till Thursday," she said.

"What's today?"

"Tuesday."

Far out. First time I knew what day it was.

2

Once a Cop . . .

I wrote Capt Rico a letter in my head.

Hey Rico.

Dig it. They moved me. Off the critical list and out of Intensive Care. I'm in my own room now, my own semiprivate if you please, and I've got it fixed up real nice.

This here thing I'm in is my Stryker frame. Every four hours they spin it around and turn me over. But I got it fixed up with this mirror so I can watch TV on my stomach.

Next to me here is my FM/AM stereo cassette player. That big box there is my tapes.

My guitar is in that case. Oh yeah, a red Gibson, an old friend, of which there seems to be a distinct shortage around here.

You like the rubber vulture? The nurses didn't wanna hang it up for me, so my mother did.

And that cactus. That's mine. I already watered it this month.

As far as my head, well, y'know, the dope keep a-comin and the train keep a-runnin but my ass is out from under the shadow for awhile anyway.

Hey, where are you? How come you didn't get in to see me?

I wrote Rico a lot of letters in my head.

Not that I was lonesome or anything. I had visitors. My mother came in every day after school; I could hear her clicking down the hall every day at four, with her red spring coat, and every day a present—the cactus, or a magazine, or a Coke.

And I also had a roommate. A double hernia named Dick the Cop. Lemme tell you about Dick.

Dick was cool. My first night in the semiprivate, I was whacked out as usual on some fine legal hygienically administered dope, when this little old gray head poked itself in the door. I looked at Dick, and he looked at me, but neither of us knew her.

"Willie?" she said.

"Over here."

"I'm Mrs. Wisniewski. From the emergency room."

"Oh yeah. Were you on when they brought me in?"

"Yes, and I'm just so glad to see you made it."

"Me too."

"How are you feeling now?"

"Oh, fine. Fine."

"Strong enough to talk?"

"Sure." As it turned out, I didn't have to talk much. Just listen.

"There was quite a to-do," she told me, "that night. First they brought you in, and I could see we were in for a busy night. We had to get a neurosurgeon, and an orthopedic surgeon—you were so lucky Doctor Cagney was on call—and an abdominal man. We thought you ruptured your spleen but it was just shock."

"Oh?"

"Yes. Then they brought your friend in. What was

21

his name? You called him the Colonel or something?"

"Close enough," I told her, rather than reveal the true identity of Capt Rico of the Cough Medicine Brigade.

I'm a private in the Brigade. Strictly a volunteer outfit. I'd followed Rico around State College campus my freshman year, hoping for . . . recognition? acceptance? what? Hoping, I guess, to be like Rico and his streetwise friends. Eventually they noticed me tagging along on the fringes of the group, and, at the Capt's insistence, took me in and turned me on. First pot, of course, and then the official initiation, which involved drinking four ounces of Robitussin A-C, and lying around with a heavy body and tapioca mind for eight hours. Didn't shit for a week thereafter, but I was in. Somehow I doubt Mrs. Wisniewski would have understood.

"I remember," she went on, "there were three men holding him down on the stretcher—my he was a big strong boy—and they called more men over to help them. He had this huge gash on the side of his neck and it was positively *spurting* blood—it just missed the artery though, lucky for him—and he wouldn't lay still and let them sew it up.

"It was the strangest thing, he kept throwing them off and sitting up and asking for your jacket. Well, we thought he must have been cold—shock, you know—and they put a half-dozen blankets on him—used up a whole night's supply of clean blankets, got them all bloody—but he said no he had to have your jacket. He said he promised you he'd take care of it for you. He said he couldn't let you down, and they finally had to give it to him just to calm him down before he lost too much blood, even though I told them it was *totally counter to procedure.*"

"Far out."

"So what I wanted to ask you was, what do you suppose he could possibly have wanted your jacket for?"

"Beats me," I said. "Must have been out of his head."

Oh yeah. Dick the Cop. Now you might think, with him lying there after having had his intestines restuffed, that he wasn't likely to be interested in doing any sleuthing over at my part of the room. Well, you'd be wrong.

Because no sooner had that lady walked out the door than Dick leaned over to me (gingerly) and said, "What'd you have in the jacket?"

And so stunned was I, and so overcome by admiration for his sheer *professionalism*, that the truth popped out of my mouth.

"Ounce of grass."

"He switch it?"

"Yup."

"Good thing. You got enough troubles."

Like I said, Dick the Cop was cool.

Big Marie's Fabulous Lentil Soup

After the old lady was gone, I noticed Dick shifting around uneasily in his bed. "You hurting?" I asked him.

"Like a bastard."

"Me too," I lied.

"Well, let's do it." He palmed his call buzzer and ordered up another round of Demerol for us. Click click click here she comes. Who's on tonight? Aaah. Maria. Steinmetz. One of those big-breasted Jewish girls who carries herself as if her body were somehow . . . lumpy. But a sort of passive turn-on.

23

Does that sound chauvinist? Well, what can I tell you? Sex was starting to be on my mind. Occasionally. I'd caught a glimpse of my cock that afternoon—looked terrible, stretch-mouthed around the catheter, lonely too—"Hey boss did you forget about me?" Looked like it must hurt, tip red and dry, crusty and cracking, but I felt no pain.

Anyhow, two left jabs and Maria was gone. So were Dick and I. Just laid back on a pleasant nod. I lit up a Camel Filter, he a Chesterfield, and we inhaled warm and toasty for a minute.

"Hey Dick."

"Yeah."

"You get your hernias together or one at a time?"

"Together."

I waited.

"It's very embarrassing." He took a deep drag. I knew he'd tell me. "This car jumped the sidewalk over on 25-A—where it runs through town?—and it pinned some kid. I'm the first car there and I come running out and see the crowd standing there and I think Jesus what are they waiting for? And I also think, I dunno, about how, you know, mothers lift these huge boulders if their kids are pinned underneath. So between the crowd and that idiot idea—I musta read it in *Reader's Digest*—I tried to pick up the car myself. I don't know what the hell I thought, but the car didn't move and I just screamed and grabbed groin, and I see this guy coming out of the hardware store with one of those compressed air jacks. Which makes more sense, cause then you can lift the car and not have to drag the kid out . . ." He remembered in silence for a moment, then, "Hey Willie?"

"Yeah?"

"Show and tell. How about you?"

"Well, it's funny . . ." He waited. "Just tonight, when Mrs. Wisniewski was talking, some things started coming back to me. Some things I think I remember, and some I'm not sure of."

"Well, what do you remember for sure?"

"Lentil soup."

That's right, Dick—lentil soup.

First the setting sun glinting off cars on the Long Island Expressway, exit 44, a burst of speed on the straightaway, hard right on Wallace Drive, skree a controlled four wheel drift, it's famed stock car racer Junior Lewis at the wheel of his famous . . . Volvo? End fantasy. I roll sedately through the neat square lawns of Plainview. I love this cool and the long shadows of this time of day, and I wish I had a Spaldeen to pop along the sidewalk.

Outside Capt Rico's house, his little brother Frankie is playing ball on the street with three or four friends. I never saw Frankie without three or four friends. And if there are four kids and three gloves or three hockey sticks or whatever, Frankie will never be the one without the glove. Rico's the same way. Not selfish. Just survivors.

I vault up the steps, using the wrought-iron rail, and stick my head in the kitchen. Big Marie, Rico's mother, is standing over the stove, her back to me.

"Wipe your feet," she says to me, without turning around, and then calls up the stairs, "Rico, did you invite any bums for dinner?" She only talks like that to people she likes. People she doesn't like get silence

in their presence, and some vicious Italian hand gesture in their absence.

"Hi Marie," I say, "what's for dinner?"

"Lentil soup. There's not very much."

"I'll pass."

"You'll eat it and like it."

"I'll try."

Up in his room, Rico's got a new toy. He gestures
me into the room, where he's hunched over a tape recorder. This is the room he grew up in, and it doesn't
quite fit him anymore, it seems to be all corners around
him. He's a tall man, twenty-five is his age—he seems
much older than me, with his angular face and fierce
red beard covering his lantern jaw. His baby-soft brown
hair is tied back with a red bandanna, and his eyes are
bright when he looks at me.

"Willie, look at this. A Roberts. I got it off of Fat
Harry for a hundred."

"Isn't that awful cheap?"

"It fell off a truck."

"Oh. Did it get damaged?" He gave me a weird
look, and I felt doltish. "It didn't really fall off a
truck?"

"No, it *fell off a truck*."

"Oh." Turns out "fell off a truck" is Italian for
hijacked.

Then Rico goes downstairs, in answer to a yell
from his mother, and I play with the tape for a minute,
until he returns with a couple bowls of lentil soup.

Lemme see. What else? We eat. Smoke. Sing. Try
a few Lenny Bruce raps into the tape recorder. Another
joint. A few disc jockey imitations. A dialect duet of
the Cisco Kid and Pancho in simulated intercourse. We

26

smoke another number. Then Rico suggests a ride. A mystery ride. He'll drive.

"Shit no, man. I gotta know where we're going."

"Lemme surprise you."

"I gotta know."

"Okay, it's a cemetery."

"Far out. I love cemeteries." We roll a couple joints for the road, I put what's left of my oh zee in my pocket, and we bound down the stairs, through the kitchen ("Where are you going?" "Out." "Why do I bother to ask?"), out to my car, I toss him the keys, and we're off.

My Demerol was starting to come on good, and I was nodding off into my thoughts.

"Is that all you remember?" asked Dick.

"Just about. The rest is mostly pictures. But I'll have to ask Rico what happened for sure."

"Where is Rico?"

"Beats me."

"I think he's a bastard for not coming to see you."

"No man, really, it's all right. Really. G'night."

"G'night."

Wake Up, Break Up

Good morning, sunshine. My I feel good this morning. Ready to uh rock and roll.

Seven pills this morning. With a glass of juice— Miss Di Costanza knows my habits. I get them all down without choking. I even pass up my shot this morning, cocky bastard that I am. Then hard on her heels comes Dr. Cagney.

He looks like Cagney, too, but even more like

Van Heflin. Short man, long strides, red hair, surgical greens. He's the orthopedic surgeon.

"How ya doin, Tiger?" Same question every morning.

"Far out. I mean it. Best I felt since I been here."

"Great. Because we got big plans for ya."

"Fantastic. So when can I sit up? When can I get a real bed instead of this rack?"

"Right after the operation."

Eration ration ation shun un. The world screeched to a halt for a minute, and outside my window the birds stopped singing. "Operation?"

"Spinal fusion. Nothing to it. We take a little bone from here, put it there, sew you up. No problem."

"Do you have to?"

"Tiger, you got five vertebrae in your back that look like kindling wood. Shoulda done it right away, but we were afraid we'd lose you."

"When are you gonna do it?" I asked in the smallest goddam voice I ever heard.

"Tomorrow."

"Tomorrow?" somebody yelled. "Why the hell didn't you tell me? Give me some time to get ready or something."

"You're ready."

"Well, give me time to get psyched up or something. I mean . . . Jesus . . . I . . ."

"Okay, Tiger, tomorrow." He straightened up and strode out of the room with a quick nod to Dick. I looked over to my left, to Dick, and he looked over to his right, to me.

"Don't tell me," he said, and reached for his buzzer to order up more dope. I nodded out the rest of the morning.

3

The Road at Twilight

They invented this shot that makes you *want* to get cut. It makes you fall in love (with everyone) and trust (anyone) and makes your soul come all over the clean white sheets.

It's made up of Demerol and Valium and scopolamine, some places, and it's called the twilight shot. They give it to everybody before operations, and if they ever gave it to you, I hope they gave you enough to get you off.

You got to know I was *behind* that stuff early the next morning.

Preop. Wave after wave of gentlest velvet satisfaction. The peace of the womb. Nurses come and nurses go. I choose not to notice. I choose to feel so good. I have found the perfect high, I think. Then:

"Hey Willie!" I awaken to find Capt Rico looming over my bed.

"They just gave me a preop shot," I tell him.

"I know that one. A real Death Trip."

"That explains a lot."

Then he says, "Sorry I haven't been around."

"That's okay."

I try to clear my head with a shake, fat chance, and look around my room. Dick the Cop is sitting up in bed in his blue pajamas with gold piping, eating his breakfast.

"Dick," I say, "this is my friend Rico," and Rico walks over to his bed. "Dick," Rico repeats to fix the name in his head, and sticks out his hand.

"Hi," says Dick. "My name's Dick, too."

"No, I'm Rico," says Rico.

"Oh, I thought you said you were Dick?"

"No, you're Dick."

"I . . . I know."

Then Rico walks back to me, leans over, and whispers, "I think that guy's a cop."

"He is," I tell him, then start to nod off.

"I'll wait here," Rico mumbles, and pulls a chair over to the window.

There must have been a godawful back-up in the OR, because when I opened my eyes again, Dick and his tray were gone—the tray to the kitchen, I imagine, and Dick to parade his hernias and shapeless seersucker hospital robe up and down the hall. The tide of pleasure came in again then, and I closed my eyes once more, not to reopen them until the man in green showed up with a gurney. Capt Rico walked me down to the elevator.

"Rico," I asked through the haze, "the accident. What happened?"

"Willie," he said, "we ran out of road."

Why Does a Blind Man Cross the Road?

While they're operating on me, let me tell you a story. Sort of a bit of background for what's gonna happen when I wake up, back in Intensive Care.

In another hospital, I had a friend, a handsome, handsome boy, a blind paraplegic spade, who was in love with the sweetest, ugliest nurse in the hospital. Now, I guess because he didn't mind she was ugly, she didn't mind his being a blind paraplegic spade; anyhow, they hit it off real well.

One night, late, I heard them making it down at the other end of the almost deserted ward, and it was sweet. I mean, the only possible visual equivalent to the sound of them balling would have to be, oh, Mick Jagger making it with Helen of Troy.

He used to ask me what she looked like a lot—I should have told him the truth, I guess, but I used to spend a lot of time evading; one day, in the course of some heavy evasion, we got to sharing some postoperative reminiscences.

"Can you remember how you wake up, man?" he said to me. "Say you just had some operation, and it about hurt to kill you, just to breathe? And the next thing you know, some fuck come walking over and tap you on the shoulder and say, 'Cough!' Later for that shit, man, the last time I got cut I asked him if he was crazy or what. I mean, I might be blind, but I got eyes. What I remember best, though, was when I woke up the day after that hit on the head . . ."

"Right," I broke in excitedly, "I remember that feeling. You know, you wake up at zero fucking hour. I mean, you start all over again, from zero, only you can't move half your body."

"Fuck that shit, man," he said to me. "I couldn't move and I couldn't talk. I could hear, but I didn't like what I was hearing."

"Jesus Christ, what'd you do?"

"I didn't *do* nothing. I went back to sleep. And

every time I woke up, I'd go back to sleep, and after about a week they operated on me again so I could talk, and I figured it was okay to wake up."

Which just about puts into perspective how I felt when I woke up after that spinal fusion.

Throwing Up Absurd

"Where's Hazel?" I meant to ask. Because when I opened my eyes, Chalice was there.

But when I opened my mouth to speak, it hurt so bad I decided to ask for some dope.

"Pain," I said. That's the way you ask for dope in a hospital. You just say you hurt, and they give you the dope like it was *their* idea.

I don't want to bore you with how bad it hurt, but I sorta have to make a point so you can appreciate what's coming. So . . . it really hurt. Worse than I could remember. And it hurt too much to even take your breath to scream, so you just whimper.

You can imagine with what relief I saw Chalice scurrying to my bedside with a needle. I felt the beautiful pain of the needle, and I had but a minute to wait before that sweet high rolled on in, a minute that I intended to use smiling at Chalice. But as I turned my head toward her, the goddamnedest thing happened.

I vomited.

"eeeeeee"

That's the sound a shriek makes when it's stuck inside your head. It doesn't quite equal the pain that comes from throwing up when the pain from breathing is already more than you can stand, but it's the best I could do.

I didn't even have the sense to pass out. I just lay there with this foolish old drunk's mantra in my head—"If you feel sick don't keep it in. Just throw it up and start again"—but there seemed to be some flaw in that logic, a flaw that tapped feebly at the back of my brain while Chalice dabbed futilely at the green bile on my face and bedding. Futilely because as she sopped up the vile stuff, I vomited again, some small warning this time—oh gawd I'm going to throw up . . . how bad will it hurt this time?—but there was nothing I could do, and I heaved again. And again. Pain became a roaring in my head, and it seemed to me I could hear every noise in the room, water taps, and bedsprings, arrhythmic sick breathing of the patients, rubber-soled footsteps, all shrieking and shrilling and scraping and clanging, and there were a thousand little voices screaming in my head.

At some point I passed out, and the noise turned ghastly, the voices wailing and groaning counterpoint to my dreams. Strange dreams. Driving down Shore Road with Nita, in the dark, snow falling silently outside the car. I have one hand on the wheel and the other inside her blouse, she has a hand inside my pants, but no sound other than screeching voices.

Then there are doctors crowded around the bed, peering intently at me, looking for something, and before I vomit again, I see Marley's ghost in the white-coated bunch, rag tied around his head, hideous fallen lantern jaw propped on Dr. Da Silva's shoulder. Out of his gaping mouth come the damned voices.

Then I'm crawling through jungle slime, beside a foul stream in a deep forest, dragging skinny skeleton legs behind me, while in the trees birds scream with human throats.

I felt—dream? real?—another needle in the wasting flesh of my upper arm, and everything grew slower, heavier, and as the voices slowed, deepened, stopped like a phonograph when you pull out the plug, I felt an old man with long stringy hair and porcupine bristle beard climb into bed with me. "It's all right," said Chalice, "he just wants to rest." We fell together into a black, dreamless sleep.

Spinning

Turns out what happened was I'd pulled an allergic reaction to the morphine they'd given me after the fusion, and had gone into shock, and nearly down the tube.

That's why I'm back in Intensive Care. I've been here a few days, will be here a few more. I suspect I'm out of danger. But danger's a meaningless quantity now, and I feel like some old saint in a picture, all arrow-pierced and torn, in sagging, limp resignation.

There's Demerol to ease the big pains. But I don't even know if I have big pains any more, it's the little ones I lie with each bad-smelling day and endless evening.

If I could only move a little, turn on my side to ease the ache in my hips, raise my head to look around, to eat.

But no, for four hours I lie flat. And then, every four hours, they spin me around, like a goddam spitted chicken. They clamp a stretcher on my front and rotate me horizontally in one sickening 180° arc, then I lie for four hours on my stomach, head down, staring through a small oval cutout just a little smaller than my face.

Four is the magic number. Four hours my face aches, and my knees, and the hipbones in front. There are phantom stabbing pains in my legs too, down the inside of my calves, whether I'm face up or down. My arms, in the crooks of my elbows, backs of hands, wrists, forearms, are bruised green and yellow from old IV's, bruised purple and blue from more recent ones. My veins keep collapsing, and every day or so, I know, will come the horror of that slow, slow stabbing and needle twisting to find a vein for the IV.

I think I have the IV because I'm not eating—anyway, I don't remember eating lately. Time passes in long hazy intervals, time between injections, between sleeps, between bedbaths, mostly in four-hour turning-over segments.

My dreams are strange, disoriented, choppy, constantly interrupted, and after awhile waking daydreamy drug dreams further blur the separation between the conscious and subconscious worlds.

Oliver Twisted

"My, you've lost some weight," said the nurse's aide. I was back in my semiprivate, and we were going through the morning wash-up.

"Yeah, I suppose so. I was always too fat anyhow." She smiled, oh my we're so brave, but I really meant it, in a dreamy sort of way, because right at that moment I was feeling pretty detached from my body. My head felt good, doped up, some spring sun shone in the window, glinted off the warm, soapy water and the shiny basin. This was the other side of the coin from the pain, from immobile aches, this was the no-body feeling. And why not? I mean, here was this pleasant-faced girl, soaping my feet, threading a washcloth between my toes, and if I looked away, I couldn't tell what she was doing.

I had to look away, mostly—you get dizzy looking at your toes from flat on your back. Everything, it seemed, conspired to make me ignore my body: the dope, the staff, the service which made movement superfluous.

And the information the staff supplied me with helped fuzz over my future. Yeah, I'd broken my back, but I'd not severed the spinal cord, nerves were known to regenerate, I was going to be fine.

Sure, I couldn't feel my legs, nor move them, but like the old joke, thank God I didn't have to.

So what to do? Watch TV, wait for injections, nibble off otherwise neglected meal trays, chat with my mother.

My mother would be in every day after school, with faculty-room gossip. I took her presence, I suppose, for granted, but her visits, presents, were milestones in my day. She wore bright clothes, smiled, walked with a springy step. I don't know where she was putting her sorrow, except maybe in her hair, which, red from birth, brown at middle age, had grayed after my father died, and now seemed white sometimes when I looked at her over a visiting-hours gin hand. I played lying flat, of course—it didn't help my game any.

I had a few other visitors from college—a couple of girls I knew, a creative-writing teacher who had warned me long ago about what he perceived as a self-consciously romantic self-destructive relationship between me and Rico. He stayed for an hour—mostly we talked about his slipped disc.

Oh, and I had one, only one, visit from Capt Rico himself, my very first night out of Intensive Care. He seemed tall, standing over the bed, rough too, and dirty, out of place—denim blue in a white world. But it felt good to hear his voice.

"So how you feeling?" the Capt asked.

"Pretty good. Weak as a kitten. Like, umm, does David Copperfield, no, Oliver Twist, yeah, he recovers from some fever and wakes up all pale, with the sun shining in?"

"In the movie."

"Well, that's how I feel."

"Strong enough for a little excitement?"

"Anything I can do lying on my back."

"Solid." Rico hung his worn suede jacket over a chair and took a foil-wrapped lump from his pocket. Then he whispered, "Oh shit, is that cop still over there?" pointing over his shoulder to the other bed, with the curtains drawn around it.

"No, he went home. That's whatsisname. He ain't wrapped too tight. Old. Very old."

"Think he'd mind . . . ?" He unwrapped the foil.

"Mind? Shape he's in we could use him for an ashtray."

"Awright. We'll do some now, and I got some rolled in a poof for later."

"Been a long time since I been high," I ventured.

"Bullshit, man, you haven't been straight since you been here."

"Well, on smoke."

"Well," he mimicked, "take a look at this."

He placed a gummy black nugget in my hand, and I brought it up to my face, examined it, sniffed it, dug at it with a thumbnail. "Don't tell me. I'll get it. Aaah, Afghani . . . Black Afghani . . . Opiated."

"Château d'Abdul, '49. An unprepossessing little number, but it'll knock you on your ass."

It's not easy to smoke a hash pipe lying on your back, but I managed. Together we watched the blue smoke curl lazily up past the bobbling rubber vulture hung from the Stryker frame, up through the semi-darkness to the ceiling. Rico kept filling the pipe as often as we emptied it, and as we smoked, I snuggled back into the dark folds of my mind, and smiled. It seemed to me I might as well be strapped down to a hi-g antiacceleration couch in a starship flaring through black space shot with pinpricks of stars gleaming in every color of the spectrum, gleaming green and yellow and blue in the utter blackness of space.

4

Shooting Fish

Awright. Awright. Awright.

Sonofabitch, things are starting to move. Starting to get some action.

Cachung, cachung, cachung. Whirr. Click. Repeat.

I lie naked save for a lead groin guard in a cold dark room while overhead this great gray machine slides and clicks into position over my belly, and takes its pictures of my innermost secrets. Cross sections of my spine at intervals of millimeters, the technician explained to me.

"Now . . . ?" I ask, when it's over.

"We wait. Comfortable?"

"Cold." So he piles some blankets on me, no pillow, and I lie on the dissecting room slab while they send the pictures out to the drugstore. He's back in five.

"Everything come out all right?"

"Perfect. Kid, you're gonna be a star."

I laugh. "Far out. I go back, now?"

"One more set."

"You paparazzi are all alike." He laughs. My we're

all having a jolly good time here in X-ray. "What now?"

"IVP. Kidneys."

"Shoot."

"Not so fast." He goes out, returns with an eleven-year-old doctor, who asks me if I'm allergic to fish. What the hell, lunch? No, I'm not.

"Okay, now, just a little pinprick." The prick. He pulls out a Buntline Special, injects about a quart of clear fluid. I feel the taste of fish behind my tongue. "Let us know if you feel nauseous." That's all I need to hear. I can feel the bile rising in the back of my throat, and gesture wildly with my spare arm. The tech rushes over with a spleen-shaped basin and sets it next to my head. The nausea leaves, and I feel slightly light-headed.

"Hey, I didn't know you could get high from shooting fish."

"You can't," says the kid doctor, who, obviously no longer needed, goes back to the closet where they keep him, to wait for the next IVP.

"It's a secret," the tech confides, then calls out from ambush, behind a lead screen, "Deep breath . . . hold still . . . Okay—breathe."

"How come you get to hide behind a screen?"

"I already got a two-headed kid," he answers. "Wait here."

You're probably wondering why I'm so goddam cheerful today. What can I tell you? Looks like I'm getting out.

Chortle.

Dr. Cagney was in to see me this A.M.

"Morning, Tiger, got a minute?"

Grumble.

40

"You getting bored with us yet?"

Peer through veiled eyelids, a noncommittal grunt. I don't trust him since the last surprise party we had, since the morphine fuckup. Like him, yeah—trust him, no.

"Got plans for ya."

"Yeah?"

"Gonna take some X-rays this morning, and if the fusion looks okay, we'll put you in a body cast and ship you out of here. You're just not sick enough to be stuck here."

"Where'm I going?"

"Well, we talked it over with your mother, and we're gonna send ya to a state rehab hospital. They'll get you on your feet again."

"Will I be able to walk?"

"Why not?"

"How about the catheter?"

"First things first. See ya after X-ray."

"Later."

"Tomorrow, Tiger."

Cast Party

So my good mood continued through the next day, which dawned hot. The hottest June day in the memory of God. And in the morning, with the flaming sun, came my red-headed doctor.

"Hey, Tiger," he said. "Hot day."

"Hot day."

"How'd you like to spend the morning in a nice air-conditioned room?"

"Say what?"

"The X-rays. Looked fine. You're about ready for some plaster."

"Oh golly." But I was pleased.

When I was a kid, I played the bouncing-the-ball-off-the-roof game. There were dozens of players, teams, a league, a world series. Rookies with Ivy League names, beloved veterans (Willie Nasaw was the Mickey Mantle of the game), wise old Puerto Ricans, brash kids—I played them all. I would set up barriers to stand for the outfield wall; an occasional boomer, when I caught the roof just right, would threaten its way toward home run territory, and I would be forced to make fantastic, suicidal, Pete Reiser catches. One such catch cost me a broken arm and collarbone, and I was in a cast for three months.

I got lots of attention, missed lots of homework, and kept the cast on until it rotted and fell from my shoulder. I dug it.

Oh yeah, the game. Since I was the only player, the game was in rather serious danger of dissolution with me out. So I figured out an equivalent with dice, kept the league together, and interviewed myself several times a week: "Tell the fans how you broke your arm, Willie." "Well, Vin, it was in the ninth inning, that series with the Pirates . . ."

So a cast for me was not a step into the teetering unknown, but a replay of old childhood karma. I thought.

Stretcher riding is a gas. When I go through the crowds of visitors I give a brave smile like I got leukemia but it ain't a-gonna get me down. It inspires them.

I am taken not to the plebian cast room (that's for outpatients) but to the OR, which is, after all, air-conditioned. I am wrapped in layers of soggy cloth and papier-mâché. It is still warm and dries on me, a prodigious hump-chested, nip-waisted white monstrosity, with pressure points on the collar and pelvic bones in front and the small of the back. My cock, still sprouting its rubber tube, lies just south of the colossus, and I notice now how thin and white my legs are before they cover me up and wheel me back downstairs.

People now glance at my humped form beneath the sheets, and quickly look away. I reach around the cast, and put my hands to my crotch, so that the strangers in the hall see some sort of misshapen dwarf with a great hard-on. Still, despite all the entertainment, I am grateful to get back to my room and find my things waiting for me, all around my bed, like my toys waited for me when I was a child.

But when I returned to my room, it was to find that the Fates—with that quirky sense of humor which had earlier in time revealed itself to the inmates of Auschwitz who were ready for a nice hot shower—had prepared a surprise for me. For I slowly came to the realization, with a mounting sense of dread, that I was trapped in this heavy shell on the hottest day in God's memory. I had been immune to the weather for so long, the shock alone like to killed me. I couldn't eat lunch, couldn't scratch the itches that accompanied the rivulets of sweat that turned my torso into a sauna.

I told no one. It was a matter of pride to me that I did not complain about small things. At that point it was one of the few remaining sources of pride I had.

Ming the Merciful

Do you by any chance remember the Ming craze of a few years back? If you saved your roaches and eventually had about an ounce of them, you would empty them all, and smoke what you got, and know it was good; and it was called by the name Ming I. Then you'd take all the roaches from Ming I and smoke them and know it was better; and it was called Ming II. And Ming II would beget Ming III; and IV and V might eventually be reached if you kept replenishing Ming I and were a fruitful head.

My last night in Farmington Community Hospital, I wrapped my lungs around a poof, which in this case was a joint consisting of pieces of the Black Afghani rolled in Ming III Roach Powder.

I lay on my back in the darkness, reveling in the luxury of a real bed (no need for the Stryker, what with the cast) and a pillow. I had been watching television, but now I lay back in the darkness, shutting off the ghost gray light of the tube, the disembodied voices from the pillow speaker; and I fired up the last half of that poof.

I swam in the glorious wood smoke smell and noticed the arrhythmia of my breathing, took too big a toke and watched the smoke my lungs could not hold float toward the ceiling and out of sight.

I was trying to make my mind be still, empty, was trying, in fact, like that old Zen koan, not to think of a white horse. ("Very good chance just crutches and leg braces," Cagney had said this morning.) I tried not to think of the men I have seen, tottering on steel crutches, dragging useless legs.

But I had no mind-clearing mantra then, with which to drive out the evil thoughts, so I set that little cricket voice in my head to talking about the delicious scene last night, and I drifted off to sleep as the projectionist ran that reel.

It's mostly a monologue. By Nurse Steinmetz. I described her earlier. You could look it up.

The scene is my asshole.

No, really.

Every week somebody digs around up there to extract two or three little marbles that my body has reluctantly decided to relinquish back to the ecology. The task usually fell to a male aide (you'll just have to use your imagination) but this night the more or less beauteous Maria asked whether I minded if she did it. Seems they were shorthanded.

Now, the lights are down, old Morris is asleep, and this girl is reaming me out, but I'm afraid I'm setting you up for a fall. Because nothing happened. Except she talked to me while she worked. In an absolutely conversational, pleasant chat voice.

She told me that I was probably wondering about what my sex life was going to be now that . . . Well, she knew a lot of people thought a paraplegic couldn't have sex but . . .

This all went right by me. I mean, nobody'd mentioned the word paraplegic to me before, and I just didn't connect it to me. So I couldn't figure out why the hell she was telling me all this, as she fooled around with a gloved hand in my ass and went on to talk about her husband.

How he was a paraplegic, but every night he'd lie on his back . . .

45

This is very embarrassing.

And she'd rub him all over with her breasts and lick his nipples and then trail down over his belly . . .

I can't go on.

I still don't know whether this was supposed to be some kind of therapy, or if she was a weird chick, but it was a very strange scene.

I loved it.

5

Famous Cripples Rehabilitation Center

A room full of crippled children. A world of crippled children. All the crooked children in the world in a room. Legless toddlers. Bowing bones. Insistent, unintelligible cerebral palsy. Gunshot paraplegics. The firecracker-maimed.

The walls are institution green, the floors yellowed linoleum. The beds are old, with iron-barred heads and feet, two rows along either wall down the length of the room.

What daylight there is in the high-ceilinged room comes through arched, wire-latticed grilled windows. Old-fashioned iron radiators are set beneath every other window.

Had quite a ride up here—no siren, but the red light flashed all the way. One disquieting thing, though. Just before they rolled me out of my room, the day nurse, Miss Keller, a quiet woman—we'd hardly spoken—stuck a few codeine pills in my hand, mumbling that she'd heard they don't give anybody any dope *up there*. What the hell?

I swallowed the first of the c's as the children

crawled, limped, swarmed spastically around my bed.

"Uh ahhenhhed?" asked one of them, an imp with a cleft palate and hairlip that split his head near in half.

"He wants to know what happened," said a boy with curly black hair that fell over his forehead in bangs. He tapped me insistently with an arm that ended neatly in a little nub at the wrist.

"My back. I broke it."

"A paraplegic," he explained seriously to the other children. They nodded knowingly.

Good kids, they were. They decided I must be tired and left me alone, trying to absorb this new world.

"This is only temporary," the admission secretary had said, "until we get an open bed in the Young Adults Ward."

"That's not our general policy," said the head nurse when I asked for something for pain. "You can ask the doctor when you see him. Not that he'll give you anything."

"We know *your* kind," said the attendant.

"One last high," I said to myself and, in a not uncharacteristically rash gesture, swallowed the remaining two pills.

And as the afternoon struggled on and the last daylight crept out the windows, I fell into a mean, mean nightmare.

Mean because it was so fucking real. About a once-seen terror that had haunted my childhood. About the Times Square Cripple.

Just Earning a Living: The Times Square Cripple

The most terrible sound in Times Square late at night is the whirr of roller skate wheels.

Almost deserted streets, lone pimps and prowlers in doorways, darkness and cold bluish neon alternating in the flash of seconds. The land where death don't have no mercy? Electric buzz, splash of lonely cars, your own footsteps falling loudly on city ears unaccustomed to the quiet.

Then, a block behind you, the faint whirr and click of ball bearings. You don't look behind you to see the legless man on his cart, but you can hear the sound louder, nearer, tempo picking up, closing faster than you can with dignity walk.

He is a jackal, this Times Square Cripple, he smells the weak ones, the ones who won't kick an importunate cripple off his cart, he smells *you,* and unless you break and run, you will feel a tug, a great tug, at your pants leg, or the hem of your skirt. (Pretty girl, his reach extends to the highest hem of your shortest skirt, and you will—oh special prize!—feel thick filthy fingers on your thigh.)

You're caught now, unless you wear breakaway football togs, and you look down into the vilest face that ever you have seen—yellow stumps of teeth, dirtier than your feet have ever been, red slit eyes leaking pus at the corner; and the voice that croaks up at you is filled with the hate that the undead feel for the living.

And unless you are one to sit alone in a ground floor room at midnight, see a leprous face (sudden, silent, grinning) at the window, and never flinch, then you had best empty your pockets for the Times Square Cripple, or he will never let you go.

I keep trying, unsuccessfully, to think of some clever way to describe the pain. It was just pain, that's all. Started that first night.

That first nighttime.

There are murmurings, rollings, scratching in the dark—the crippled children sleep, each in a position dictated by incapacity. The little fella to my left lies dead still on his back—he's learned to lie still, even in his sleep, so as not to twist his shriveled lower limbs too hopelessly.

The boy to my right was once, he told me (I think) a real muscular dystrophy poster boy, but now, in the dark, his body turns restlessly, tensely distorted by the pull of muscles dragging unevenly.

Me? I lie here patiently, on my back, a turtle up-ended. I must call for help to turn to either side (to untwist my legs, which drag behind like lost babies, to unfoul my tubing). That means lighting the red bulb over my bed and waiting for the attendant making hourly rounds to notice the light. So it's best not to want to turn over.

And the pain has begun. Objectively speaking, it's not too bad as yet—paresthesia, phantom pains that originate in the once-mashed spinal column, but are felt in the legs as stabbing pains. Like being cut with a hot knife.

But the worst is the panic. A fevered panic, as I wonder how bad the pain will get. I had for a month been taking the Demerol as much from fear of pain as from pain itself. I can feel hysteria slouching, irresistible, toward consciousness, toward terror, until I can no longer distinguish fear from pain, and the wheezings and murmurings of the tormented children are the soundtrack. Time passes slowly here in the Famous Cripples Rehabilitation Center, but the night goes.

Feeya Itself, and Paul Biloxi

The morning, as mornings are, was lighter, and I brightened up considerably. As one famous cripple said, "The only thing we have to feeya is feeya itself."

For one thing, I'd made it through the night. I didn't necessarily look *forward* to another one, but I could make it if I had to.

For another, the head nurse promised they would move me into the Young Adult Ward that afternoon.

Then too, the kids were mostly all out for therapy, or school, and the solitude was heartening.

And there was entertainment. It came crashing down the hall and past my bed at forty-five-minute intervals. Its name was Paul Biloxi, and he hated his legs. Hated them. And they hated him.

First time I saw him, he stumped down the hall past me, cursing his legs. The second time he stopped at the metal chair by my bedside for a rest. He didn't rest much.

"My name is Paul Biloxi," he said. "From Hammond, Indiana." He paused, looked down thoughtfully. "I think the left one's too short."

I looked down my body to see if he was talking about me, but then I saw him kneading his thighs with his fists.

"I wouldn't know," I said.

"No, it's definitely the left one, goddam sonsabitches, they can send a man to the moon, you'd think they could learn to build a leg . . . Well, I gotta be going."

I dunno, they looked like all right legs to me: flesh-colored, some sort of supersynthetic material, detachable with shoes and socks to save bending over.

On his next trip, forty-eight minutes later by the watch I kept next to my bed, he came galumphing down the hall, kicking his legs out and using two metal canes like ski poles. He sat down again, letting the canes crash to the floor, and said, "Not only is the left one too short, it's heavier than the right one." Tears of rage came into his eyes, and he asked, "How the hell can I walk if they don't *build* the goddam things right."

He struggled to his artificial feet then, and took off again, to be followed within five minutes by a harried-looking physical therapist.

"Which way did he go?"

"I don't know," I lied, never wont to turn somebody in, "but he looked pretty upset."

"Yeah, he's supposed to go home to Indiana tomorrow, and he just can't face that this is the best he can hope for."

I disagreed. "It may be the best he's gonna *get*, but it ain't the best he can *hope* for."

"Anyhow, I gotta find him before he chafes his stumps all up, and has to stay here till they heal. He did that two weeks ago."

"He went thataway," said I. Back to Indiana, Paul Biloxi. Sink or swim.

My Friend Melonhead

And who is this man-boy who sits by my new bed in the Young Adult Ward? He has just gone through the elaborate ritual of lighting a cigarette with his only usable hand: holding the pack between his knees, extracting one Camel, placing it between his lips, bending one match down from the pack and with a thumb striking it, then shaking the whole book to extinguish the match.

He offers the cigarettes to me, and we smoke together in silence for a moment. His head looks like a melon with a slice gone and the skin healed over. Just a great deep furrow scored down the upper left skull.

His speech, when at last he speaks to me, is largely unintelligible, a palsied drawl with a nervous stutter. I can understand him only by staring deep into his eyes, and nodding or shaking my head in almost constant feedback, depending on whether I have understood him or not.

"Scared?" is his first question, and when I understand him, I say no, I'm fine, but since we are looking into each other's eyes he knows I'm lying.

"It's not so bad here," he says. "Just take it slow."

"Slow?"

"There's nothing you can *do*," he says, softly as always. "Just wait it out."

We are alone in the ward. The boys, he informs me, will be back soon.

His name is Frederick, and he says it in full, though apparently it is a difficult word for him. He is my cubicle mate, the ward being divided by low wood and glass partitions into two-bed cubicles.

"Wait what out?" I ask him. He shrugs one shoulder, his good left one, and takes a deep drag of his smoke.

"The rest of our life," he says then, and when at last I understand him, he breaks out into a lopsided grin.

Just as we finish our cigarettes, the doors at the end of the ward open, and the young adults come crashing in in a tangle of wheelchairs, carts, crutches and bodies, acting very much like the Bowery Boys under instructions to improvise. Frederick withdraws to his own bed to watch the fun.

There is a game of saluggi in progress. A blue Yankee cap is making erratic progress around the room, followed not very closely by a CP named Jack.

The cap is, as they enter, in the possession of a fat black boy in a wheelchair. Joel? Joel. Both his legs end at the thighs. As Jack nears him, he yells "saluggi!" and tosses the cap behind him, to another boy. Jack staggers toward *him*, jaws working, drooling, saying gimme, in a twisted howl, like a 45 record at 33 1/3. But before he can reach his hat, the other kid ducks away, and passes it on.

You know the game. Maybe you called it keepaway.

It goes on for another ten minutes. Jack works himself up pretty good, lumbering from bed to bed, one step behind his cap; curses tear themselves from his lips, and at one point somebody yells at him, Watch out you don't fall and hit your head, Jack, you might get cerebral palsy.

There's some far out razzle-dazzle work with that cap, let me tell you, some Meadowlark Lemon hidden hand fakes, some Bob Cousy behind the back passes, until finally the hat reaches Frederick's bed, and he lets it lie there until Jack reaches it and replaces it on his head, where apparently it almost always resides.

The game is over, the shouting dies, and the crippled boys' attention turns to me.

"This is Willie," says Frederick, and they seem to have no trouble understanding him.

"Pleased to meetcha," I say, and some of them nod or speak; others stare thoughtfully at me and turn back to their own beds and business.

The Bedchamber of the Royal Cripples

At dinner time, an aide rolled by with a heavy steel cart cast off by Horn and Hardart.

He slipped a gray hamburger into a cold bun. With a deft twist of a scoop he dished out a lump of greenish mashed potatoes. He sloshed out a cup of Kool-Aid. Bug juice. He flipped a ladle full of dessert into a bowl. Looked like stew. Apple Brown Betty.

Then he handed me the tray like he expected me to eat the slop.

Bet your ass I didn't.

But here, a hundred miles from home, there was no nurse to get me a sandwich on her break, no mother to bring me goodies. So, like a wicked child, I went to bed hungry.

To bed, I say, though I was already in one. But not to sleep. For after precisely the half-hour that I had been warned to stay still for, the head nurse decided we were cool and split for the night, leaving us in charge of Short Fat Fanny.

Who promptly made one quick pass of the ward,

and, on the return leg of her tour, stopped briefly to scoop up DeWitt, her lover, the blind black paraplegic I told you about, who was already in his wheelchair, waiting, and she returned with him to the nurses' room at the end of the hall.

Then, a short hush. The moonlight has slipped in the high grilled windows and creeps silver along the floor. Short Fat Fanny and blind DeWitt have their secret grope on the sprung red leather couch in the nurses' office. And the wheelchairs pass through moonlight and darkness to gather around my bed, muffled rubber wheels on the floor, and the clickclickclick of Billy's wheelchair with the plastic spinners and streamers in the spokes are the only sound.

Eager whispers around my bed.

"Who's got the dope?"

"Hey Willie."

"Hey."

Then the good rich smoke billows up into the moonlight, as one, two, many joints go around the cripples' circle. Mostly silence, indrawn breath, explosive coughs, giggles. Moonlight full in the bedchamber of the royal cripples, and here—yes, the perfect touch— steel pincers handle the joint firmly, delicately as a diamond cutter's vise.

"Robo, the Living Roach Clip."

"A slave to his master's vice."

"Chopped off his hands cause he always dropped the roaches."

"Poor bastid."

And then some of the usual. What happened to you? Rolled a car. What happened to you? Subway.

"No shit, Joel?"

"Subway ran over me."

"Yeah right. You were just standing in the station and the AA jumped the tracks and . . ."

"Fuck off, Billy. No, Willie, I was lying on the tracks."

"Suicide?'

"Naw, somebody pushed me."

"Pushed you?"

"By accident. He kept saying he was sorry. Sorry sorry sorry."

"He probably was."

"Sheeit, not as sorry as I was."

I bet.

And so that night passed considerably easier than the first night. I thought I was slipping in pretty breezy to what I thought was to be my home for awhile.

6

Bug on a Stiff Gray Sheet

It took me no longer than the first week to discover that my new home—I'll continue to call it the Famous Cripples Rehabilitation Center, the FCRC—was a bureaucratic fraud, a torturous sieve through which someone, somewhere, had to be getting rich.

It was run by the state, and had a fine reputation for healing, for rehabilitation. "They work miracles there." It got its share, I believe, of grant money, and tax money, and had celebrities show up from time to time, to grace ceremonies.

But on my ward we were lucky to get clean sheets, which were nonetheless stiff, gray, and ripped. The food was grown on the state prison farms and processed by the prisoners. The ketchup was brown and the hamburgers pebbly with gristle.

The therapy departments were so understaffed that residents like me (killing time until our wounds healed enough for rehab proper) almost had to be reintroduced to our therapists before our occasional appointments.

The doctors buzzed by the beds twice a week on

Grand Rounds. Our intercourse with the doctors was more a matter of presentation than treatment.

And at night, when the staff was gone, came the creepy-crawlie (shh) . . . bugs.

About the night I discovered the (shh) . . . bugs:

Little Billy was a paraplegic not unlike myself. He wouldn't drink his four quarts of water a day, either (got to keep those little kidneys flushed), and one day they took him away to operate on his bladder, to remove the stones that had for a year been forming in the stagnant reservoir of urine he was unable to expel.

They rolled him back down to the ward (pale face against the torn gray sheets). There was no recovery room here, no intensive care. They gave him pain medication for exactly twenty-four hours after the operation, then cut it off cold turkey, and for the next three days snarled at him when he whimpered.

Ever had an operation? Remember how good and brave and secure you felt, even in pain, while some nurse like Chalice held water to your lips, took your vital signs every few minutes, took away your pain when she could? And your roommates whispered to their visitors, and called the nurse for you if you couldn't reach your buzzer. No one could do much for you, save let you know that they would do all they could, and that was enough.

When I am in pain, I am touched by the people who hold pain in their eyes for me.

Billy was thirteen years old, and they let him lie there and whimper. All night.

He awakened the ward with his screams at two in the morning. I hated him, briefly, for pulling me from sleep to this world, this FCRC, until I saw his pale head beating the pillow, saw his urine bottle filled with the blood and pus that are the leavings of the operation. "It's all right, Billy," I tried to whisper to him, but his bed was too far down the line. I heard the night attendant, not Fanny this night, as she whispered threats to him, to shut him up, and then turned out the ward lights again, leaving me awake now in the dark, with no chance to get back to sleep.

I slept poorly those days, and was learning (a habit that has stood me in good stead) to rest as much as possible when I could not sleep. I was, of course, not allowed to turn on a night light to read by.

So I rested, and tried to think of good times, which, so immersed was I in this new world, went back only as far as Farmington Community Hospital, to nights when I could call to a nurse for cocoa, or dope, or a kind word, nights when I was not so alone, and, in all things beyond my mind, so desperately impotent. The good thoughts soothed me, and I relaxed a bit.

Then, suddenly, I was wide awake, and all my body hairs bristled with terror. I had a sense of *not* being alone which was foreign to me in this lonely bed. Once in half-sleep, as a child, I felt a hand holding my hand, that dangled off the side of the bed. I held my breath in a silent scream for a few minutes until I fell back asleep. But my company this time was no dream phantom, but rather two, three, four, five—no, four—cockroaches crawling around the corners of my vision, brown on the stiff gray sheets. I had this strong feeling of, well, immobility. There *I* was, in my cast. And. I. Couldn't. Move.

I screamed out and wiggled a little in my cast, but my mind was dead calm, watching them. I thought

60

at first they were bedbugs that were going to bite me, down where I couldn't reach, that would eat me up where I couldn't feel, but the attendant laughed at me, they're just cockroaches, they won't hurt you, stop being a baby, don't wake the rest of the boys, they need their sleep.

It's come to this, I thought, and resolved to get the hell out of this place if I had to gnaw off a finger to do it. I believe I dreamed that night that I was worm food, dead, in my grave.

Letters, We Get Letters

I got some mail that week. A letter from Capt Rico that went as follows:

Dear Willie,

This is yr Capt speaking. As to why I haven't (ahem) been up to see you:

1) You know about my aversion to hospitals. That's part.

2) Seems my Ford is (ahh) no longer with us. Since I cracked up yr Volvo (remember that?) the master of that great greasepit in the sky has turned from intolerant to vengeful. This time, I ran, not out of road, but out of luck. Me and my brud just put this new transmission into good old Henry, & was trying it out on the Expwy? For one reason or another (could the fact that we were stoned when we installed it be a factor of contributory negligence?), the old tranny dropped when we shifted to overdrive to pass this van that was hogging the center lane. Dropped! Which tranny, fortunately, hitting which road, acted as one hell of a braking force & we excaped with minor abrujos and con-

tagions. We had to have the car put to sleep at the vets. So to get money for some new 'Wheels' (that's street talk, son):

3) I started pumping gas, at the Sunoco station near my house, where:

4) The goddamnedest thing happened. A white 'vette pulls up to the pump four nights ago (4-speed positraction, the works) & says fillitup with 260 & are you married or single? So I stop my inspection of the car (327 cubes—in that old box shape—had to be pre-62—but mint condition!) and start inspecting the driver, who turns out to be this redhead named Nora, built like a brick gas station.

We palavered a bit, reached an agreement—I'll do a valve job for her, she'll do one on me.

Remember this is the station with the Sparkling Rest Rooms! What more can I say? When this chick comes (every two minutes) she farts through her cunt—blup blup. I stopped in midfuck trying to figure out what the noise was. So:

5) I work 16 hr a day and fuck 8. As soon as I can find an extra hr or two in there, I'll be up to see you. In a white 'vette. Or else not. Whatever happens. Right? Right!

> Regards,
> Capt Rico

I answered him, briefly:

Dear Capt,

I gotta get out of this place.

I still haven't been to Physical Therapy, my legs are getting stiff. They say I got an appointment Thursday with the chief PT so she can prescribe (fr chrissakes) my treatment. Thursday!

If they don't loosen me up soon, I'll have to learn to be a plank for a living at Occupational Therapy. Which I've been to once—they turned me over on my stomach and told me to try to do this jigsaw puzzle.

Besides, whaddayawanna bet that Big Chief PT is gonna stick pins in me. That's one thing about Dr. Cagney—he tried not to stick pins in me unless he had to. They're really pin happy around here.

I want out.

Mommy.

Love,
Willie

Then I borrowed a stamp from Frederick and had him put the letter in the mail drop for me.

So . . . I did almost nothing that first week—lay on my back and read, listened to the radio, got to know my ward mates.

I suppose I was closest to Frederick. I learned from him the best way to talk with, to understand, someone with fucked-up speech. I learned to give him my fullest attention, not to withdraw myself, which was my usual way of coping, but to lean in, watch his eyes, his face, for cues to his words. I asked him what happened to him once—whew, talk about fate zigging when it should have zagged! He was mowing his stepfather's lawn when—whizz—the power mower picked up a stone, shot it into his skull. Pause for unconsciousness, pause for a couple of operations, welcome to the FCRC, Frederick. He'd been here for over a year. He'd learned patience. He told me I'd learn it too.

Fourth of July

Boy! Guess what today is! Hint: it's a holiday. Hint: it's hotter'n hell. Give up? It's the Fourth of Fucking July.

It's also Sunday, and for the past two days families have been arriving to pick up bodies that were well enough to get weekend passes. They rolled Fat Joel out of here Friday. It was his first wheelchair-to-car transfer, and I'm told he ended up on his ass, on the curb, in tears. It took his father and two strong aides to get him back up and into the car—God knows how they'll get him *out* when he gets home.

Yesterday most everybody else got themselves rolled, carried, or "assisted" to their homes, and I swear, every goddam parent that came in here to pick somebody up asked me the same question: "Goin home this weekend, son?"

"Nope, think I'll stick around here for awhile."

So there's only four of us left in this thirty-bed ward. Billy is feeling better, but he's still postop; there's a quad on a stretcher down at the other end of the ward —he don't wanna talk to anybody yet—I think I know where he's at, and leave him alone; and there's DeWitt, who's in love with Short Fat Fanny,' who, lucky for them, is on duty this deserted afternoon and evening. The others won't be back till tomorrow night, so DeWitt and Fanny are down in the nursing office, off the end of the ward, billing and cooing, and, I hope, fucking.

So, for all intense and porpoises, I am alone on the ward. Lunch, a cellophane-wrapped tuna fish sandwich, is decorated with a little paper American flag on a toothpick. I dunno, for some reason that little decorative touch (some thoughtful bureaucratic decision, no doubt), that little flag on a nearly barren tray in an empty ward, just does me in.

Are we downhearted?

You bet your ass.

Wonder what I'm gonna do?

Shit, I don't wonder at all. I know what I'm gonna do.

Right! I'm gonna get stoned, that's what. Scuse me . . .

Hot damn, that's better. Whip that black ass grinning ape name of Down.

And whip out the *Rolling Stone*. Start with the letters page.

And turn on the Ray D O. It's Dan Ingram—bitching and chuckling. And Creedence—Fogarty's voice ripping hell out of the middle of that tight ass no waste sound. There now, that's not so bad.

But—is that a train comin down the track?

No, it's Fanny pushing DeWitt. And that wheelchair. Wobbling? Or is it me?

No, here they are at the foot of my bed.

"Willie," says DeWitt, "I'm downhome, but I ain't so downhome gone I gotta git high off this garbage." He shows me a bottle of Ripple. I take a hit and hand it back.

"What can I do for you, DeWitt?"

"You got any extra weed?"

"What I bought from Joel."

"Lend me."

"You're gonna get high, Fanny?" Flipped me out!

"I'm gonna git Fanny high," says DeWitt.

"Take it with my blessing," I tell them, and hand

Fanny two j's that she puts in her uniform pocket. "And let me know how everything comes out. Or goes in."

"You don't git around much, Willie," DeWitt says, looking blindly straight down the ward. "But you don't miss much, either."

FDR

I next saw Fanny somewhere around five thirty. She brought around the dinner trays. (Two little flags now flew bravely from two uneaten tuna fish sandwiches.) She asked me if I wanted her to bring over that new quad to eat with, but I had visions of the two of us lying there silently like two beached fish, and declined, so she fed him at his bed down the ward, while DeWitt parked over by me. I watched him eat.

Après sandwich, DeWitt and Fanny and another joint disappeared back into the nursing office. My radio played low. I tried to imagine what it would be like fucking if you were blind. Then I just tried to imagine what it would be like fucking. God, I was so far away from it, I even had trouble imagining. I hoped I could fuck sometime. I wondered whether FDR could fuck. My imagination was slightly handicapped about FDR—I could only imagine him in his wheelchair.

So I imagined, in clinical detail, him and Eleanor balling in the wheelchair—I guess they'd have to take the arms off.

But as far as my mind could take me was not far enough, and the evening passed slowly. I got a bad headache from the dope and couldn't get Fanny's attention to borrow an aspirin. She came around, eventually, at ten o'clock, to turn out the lights. I tried to put myself to sleep with my sleepy-time litany: twenty-four sheets make a quire; twenty quires make a ream; two reams make a bundle; five bundles make a bale.

I find paper very relaxing, don't you?

But not relaxing enough, apparently. I couldn't sleep. I heard Billy moan, down the ward. We both lay awake, and neither of us acknowledged the other's presence.

Then, "Billy," I said, softly. No answer. "Billy," louder.

"Unh."

"How you doin?"

"Unh."

"Hurts?"

"Yeah."

"Can't sleep?"

"Unh unh."

"Wanna hear a story? "It's about somebody like us." I thought quickly. "Somebody named Bumpy."

"Yeah?"

"Yeah. He lived ten thousand years ago."

Stone-Age Cripple

"Bumpy was born with one leg six inches shorter than the other, an extreme misfortune, indeed, since among his tribe, malformed babies were generally left on a hillside to bawl while great leathern-winged scavenger birds tore them apart limb from limb.

"But Boney, Bumpy's mother, kept the babe well swaddled in eohippus hides until he was too old to abandon. In time the rest of the tribe got used to watching him bobble around the cave bump   bump

bump   bump, and as long as Boney worked extra hard, they were

67

inclined to let him mope around. They were a very liberal tribe. You know what liberal means?"

"No."

"Me either. Doesn't matter.

"They ate well, by Stone-Age standards. They foraged for truffles and rutabagas—ever had a rutabaga? —and had begun to domesticate some goat-like creatures, which were prized for their heavy, creamy milk, and were eaten after a long and full life, killing being unknown to Bumpy's people unless it was done to them.

"They probably would have eaten better if they *had* been hunters, but the only weapons they had were rocks and sticks, and they all threw like second basemen.

"Neither had they begun to cultivate any fruits or grains, having had no incentive or inspiration. Gotta have inspiration.

"Bumpy was loafing around in the cave one morning, as usual, and trying to ignore his mother's bitching, as usual.

" 'Bumpy,' Boney was saying, 'did I tell you about that tribe over by the Mojave Sea?'

" 'Only a thousand times, Ma.'

" 'Well, they have lots of cripples there, but they don't lie around all day, like you, they *contribute*. They call them artists. They paint these lovely pictures on the cave walls, buffalos and lions and people. It just does wonders for the cave, and they feel like *useful members of society.*'

"You a useful member of society, Billy?"

"Yeah."

"Me too."

"But not Bumpy. 'Aw Ma,' he said, 'I don't wanna

be a useful member of society. Anyway, I can't paint. I tried. I got no talent. My eohippus looked like a canteloupe with legs, and my people looked like bugs. Pop threw buffalo shit all over the wall when he saw my paintings.'

" 'Your father was just in a bad mood that day because he misplaced the herd.'

" 'Some herd. Four lousy goat-likes.' Whap. Boney slugged him one right across the chops.

" 'Your father and I do the best we can, which is more than I can say for you.'

" 'Aw ma.'

" 'I'll aw ma you. All right, you won't art, you can work. Starting this afternoon, you can go meet your father and help him carry back the goat-likes' milk. Three bags are too many for him. He's getting all bent over.'

" 'Ma, it's too far for me to walk. I get all tired and sweaty, and my hip hurts, and I get nauseous from all the bumping up and down.'

" 'It's not that far, you're just lazy. I admit it, it's my fault, I spoiled you, I sweated for you and foraged for you so you never wanted for rutabagas, and now, this is the thanks I get . . .'

" 'Awright, ma, I'll go. I'll go. See? I'm leaving.'

"I wonder if I'm doing the right thing, she thought, watching him jolt along over the first hill toward the pasture."

"Mothers are a pain in the ass," said Billy.

"I'm hip. Anyhow, Bumpy's father, Burny (he was a fire tender first class, and stayed outside the cave all night twice a week tending the watch fires and telling dirty jokes with his buddies. *A* dirty joke, rather—they only had one) was surprised to see his son come bumping down the slope.

" 'Hey, come to keep your old man company, hey?' He threw an arm around his son.

" 'Aw Pa,' Bumpy said, shrugging him off, 'Ma made me come. Said I was supposed to help you carry the milk home.'

" 'Wonderful woman, your ma,' said Burny. 'Glad to have you aboard.'

"Bumpy lay down in the shade while his father commenced the milking chores, which took up most of the afternoon, as they included catching the goat-likes first, then trying to hold them, milk them, and catch the milk in the goat-like-skin bags. Bumpy slept, dreaming of his soft bed back in the cave.

"Toward sundown, his father woke him. He stood up, listing sharply, and Burny hung one of the bags of milk over his low-side shoulder.

" 'We're going to have to hurry, son,' he said. 'The sun is falling fast, and Gods know what would happen to us if we got caught in the dark.'

"They both shuddered and began to climb the first of the two hills between the pasture and the cave. The father strode manfully, the son tagged along as best he could,

bump   bump   bump   bump
     bump   bump   bump   bump.

"This isn't too bad, thought Bumpy. If it keeps the old lady off my ass, it's worth it. But along about the rise of the second hill, he began to tire and fell behind.

"Boney was frantic when she saw Burny come over the hill toward her, alone.

70

" 'Where's Bumpy?' she called.

" 'Coming along, dear,' said Burny, and punched her on the arm in greeting. 'You know, trying to walk with that kid is a drag. I get all seasick, watching him bounce up and down. I think we shoulda put him out on the hill when he was born, like my mother said.'

" 'Your mother is a brontosaurus,' said Boney, rapping him on the skull with her knuckles. 'Go back and find that boy.'

"But before he could move to obey, they saw Bumpy himself come bobbling over the crest of the hill, his whole body aching, and the bag of milk feeling heavier than he ever would have believed possible.

" 'Oh Bumpy, we're so proud of you,' she said, taking the bag from him as he drew nigh.

" 'That's right son,' said Burny, taking the bag from her. 'Let's see if you spilled any.' He peered into the bag.

" 'Oh my,' he gasped.

" 'What is it?'

" 'The milk! It's all . . . thick. And yellow.'

" 'Let me see,' said Boney, yanking the bag back. 'Bleagh!'

"She stuck a finger in the mess and put it in her mouth.

" 'Oh oh oh,' said the first woman ever to taste butter, 'It's delicious!'

" 'Let me,' her husband cried; he agreed, licking his fingers.

" 'Needs salt,' said Bumpy when they let him have a taste.

"Well sir, by that very night, the whole tribe had been initiated into the delights of the new delicacy, and were practically lining up to offer their most prized shiny rocks to Bumpy if he would carry their milk back for them the next day. His afternoons were soon booked solid for the next week, and the men invited him out to tend his first fire with them that night, which was sort of like a bar mitzvah.

"But the benefits of his serendipitous discovery accrued not only to Bumpy and his tribe, but also to the human race at large, for the best minds of Bumpy's people were fixated on butter day and night.

" 'It's not quite right, there's something missing here,' was the consensus, even as they dug their greasy hands into the butter that Bumpy fetched each sundown.

"And so they thought, and talked, talked and thought, until they worked out the idea of bread.

" 'Bread and butter,' they sighed, and, inspired, began the long process of cultivation that converted the idea into a reality, and culminated in civilization as we know it.

"So remember, Billy," I said. "If it weren't for us cripples, there'd be no electric lights, and we'd all be in a cave somewhere eating truffles and rutabagas three times a day."

But Billy said nothing. He just snored.

7

Dumbbells

"Well, there's not much we can do with you till that cast comes off. Some range of motion maybe a little arm work." The chief PT shrugged.

"When will the cast come off?"

"Well," she said, turning away, "that depends on what the orthopedist says. I assume somebody wrote orders for you to see him. He comes in Fridays." Then she turned to speak briefly with a coltish young lady standing by the door.

The room I was in appeared to have been at some time or another a lovely old-fashioned solarium with high windows, shutters opening outward, on to a view of . . . what? Can't say, for now the room was criss-crossed by separating screens, and the shutters were painted institutional green, and closed.

The chief left, and the young woman came over to me.

"I'm Algie," she said. "I'll be working with you this morning."

"Are you a PT?" I asked.

"Aaah, yes."

"Where'd you train?"

There was a hierarchy in these things, I'd learned from Frederick. Rusk was supposed to be the best.

"Oh, I'm still a student. At the CCFW."

Connecticut College for Women? Community College of Fort Worth? Can Cripples Fuck Women? I wondered as she lifted up one of my legs in her hands.

She didn't quite know what to *do* with it though, and her elbows flapped aimlessly while she tried to bend my leg at the knee.

I winced, and grabbed sheet, waiting for that pain I remembered (who said you can't remember pain?) so well from Farmington. But I had a pleasant surprise coming. The leg was so stiff she couldn't bend it. She looked at it crossly for a minute, then leaned into it again. Nothing.

"Why don't you push a little harder," I suggested. "Get your shoulders into it."

"The chief warned me about forcing it. I don't know what to do."

"I won't tell if you won't."

"I'll take you outside for some sun!"

"Good therapy."

"Right." And she grabbed a pair of miniature dumbbells from the rack, stowed them between my legs on the gurney, and wheeled me on the tortuous trek to the sunlight.

Years ago, long before they had cars that could hit seventy miles per hour, this place had been somebody's country estate, and the stone great house showed signs of some respect and care. The hallway floors were laid with tiny chips of stone, the woodwork was scrolled, detailed, and there were niches where no doubt grandfather clocks and hat trees and halberds had been once.

But now it was chopped and blocked into an institution, and what had once been solemn and dignified was somber and depressing, musty. Dorms had been built perpendicular to the main house, off either rear corner, and all the buildings were connected by stone and glass corridors and tunnels.

Algie rolled me through a hall, half the width of which had been converted into PT cubicles, and down a long covered ramp on the side of the greathouse, out to a lawn. She handed me the dumbbells, and returned to get her other patients—she had three every half hour.

I looked at the dumbbells dumbly and then at her retreating back. Hey. What the hell good are these little things? They're toys.

Just for the hell of it, though, I raised one up from the shoulder.

Holy shit, these things are heavier than I thought. Far out. Must be some new metal. They feel like ten pounders, but they're the size of a new baby's arm.

I did five pumps with each arm and barely had enough strength to lower the dumbbells back to the gurney. By that time Algie had returned.

"Hey," I asked her, "how much do these things weigh?"

"Three pounds."

Fever Down in My Bones

I resolved to eat all my lunch and dinner that day and drink lots of water to stave off the bladder infection they were warning me against. My resolve lasted about two bites into the shit-colored fish sticks.

I don't know why I didn't drink the water. I never

drank the water. I'd just look at that big pitcher, and pour a glass, and sip it, and put it down.

I don't know why.

I sure didn't want to be like Billy, still lying there with a blood-filled piss bottle and whimpering now and then.

I don't know.

I started shivering. Now, let's see . . . Monday was the end of the holiday, Tuesday was PT . . . I started shivering Wednesday night.

The other kids were wandering around in underwear or pajamas, and I was shivering in my cast, beneath a blanket. Frederick noticed it first and called the aide, who stuck a thermometer in my ass and two aspirins in my mouth.

It started getting warmer. I cast off the blanket, then immediately grew colder, and Frederick helped me replace it.

The nurse who was covering our ward (and two others) came in to yell at me, showed me my urine bottle.

"Infection," she shouted. "See how cloudy it is?"

Cloudy! Sheeit, it looked like orange juice. Fresh, pulpy orange juice.

Just before bedtime, she returned with an orange and yellow capsule, two white tablets, and a small red capsule. She made me drink a glass of water with each pill. I thought I would choke to death or my stomach would split like an overfilled water balloon, but instead I began to feel better almost immediately and went to sleep.

In the morning, my urine looked more like lemonade, and I was very proud of it. I swore that I would drink until it looked like water.

I didn't.

I don't know why.

I don't.

But it worked out all right anyway. Turns out getting sick was the best thing I could have done under the circumstances.

"The very best thing," said Uncle Lou, whom my mother had summoned when she visited me Thursday and saw my weakened condition. Lou the Lawyer, he was called in the family. Lou looked like a walking Alka-Seltzer ad. The before. "I played a couple of angles here. First thing, we can get them to say you need medical attention they can't give you here. They're only too happy to get rid of you.

"The second angle is your father."

"My father? He's dead."

"I shouldn't know that, my own brother? Of course he's dead. Of a *war-related injury*."

"A heart attack?"

"He was weakened by some disease he caught down in the Philippines. Gave him chronic hypertension. It's all documented."

"Where am I going?"

"The Queens Naval Hospital. Nearer home, where your mother can visit. Then, when you're better—the sky's the limit. You're a very lucky boy."

"Why?"

"Because you're the dependent of a veteran of the U.S. Army who expired of a war-related injury. The U.S. Army takes care of its own," he said proudly.

"Cheez, I'm sorry I didn't enlist."

77

"You'll be out of here Saturday. And I'm working on the insurance money."

"Thanks, Uncle Lou."

"Don't thank me, thank your mother who had the good sense to come get me."

Thanks, Ma.

Moom Pitchers

"What's the movie tonight?" asked Frederick, combing back his hair with his good left hand, which also held his omnipresent cigarette.

" 'Farewell to Arms.' Starring Robo the Living Roach Clip," I suggested.

"Fuck you," screamed Robo from across the room.

"What's with him?"

"Oh, he's got a heavy date tonight," said Joel. "And he's nervous. He can't figure out which attachment to use."

"Didn't they give him a screw-on vibrator?"

"Shut the fuck up, Willie, or I'll nip your goddam catheter out."

"Nerves, nerves!"

Everybody did seem to be a bit keyed up for this once-a-month movie night. It was best clothes, or a clean sheet and blankets for the horizontal patients like me. The ward positively buzzed. Hair that had been uncombed for weeks was getting slicked down; there was a run on mouthwash that almost depleted the community of Lavoris; Joel even pinned the legs of his trousers where they flapped below his stumps; and one manually dextrous kid had been dispatched to the bathroom to roll joints.

Because here in the FCRC, this Friday night was movie night, was America's date night, and most of the kids had long-standing assignations with patients from the girls' wards.

Show time was eight. Long about seven thirty, DeWitt rolled over to me.

"C'mon Willie. Me'n' Fanny'll take you the long way around."

"How? Takes two just to put me on a gurney."

"Shit. Just watch her. She's fantastic."

She was, too. First she cranked my bed up to the gurney height, then slid the wheeled stretcher flush to the bed and locked the wheels. She had DeWitt sit at the foot of the bed, then handed him the urine bottle so the catheter lay straight between my legs.

"Okay, Willie. When I say go, you roll to your left and DeWitt you move the bottle a foot to *your* right. Go!"

And there I was, on my stomach, on the gurney. From there, turning to my back was easy enough—she cleared all the tubing, stowed the bottle on the rack below the gurney, and we were ready to roll.

Roll we did, down one of the darkened stone corridors that connected the ward with the main building. Through the huge windows set in arches along either side of us, we could see the night. The only light was coming from small glowing panels set near the stone floors, and I had a Gatsby summerhouse flash.

We fired up a joint outside the darkened psychiatrist's office. Fanny allowed as how she'd take a little toke, seeing as how she wasn't on duty.

"They take you to the shrink yet, Willie?" asked DeWitt.

"Unhhunh. He gave me this test where they show you pictures, you know, and you're supposed to make up stories about them. (Hssss inhale.) Every picture I made up had the most horrible Alfred Hitchcock story I could think of. Like he'd show me a picture of a gray-haired old lady and a little kid, with a Norman Rockwell dad coming into the room, only the faces are all shadowy. So I told him the daddy just came in from outside (hsssss inhale hack hack exhale) where he dug a grave for the kid and they were going to put the kid in the oven and kill it.

"Every picture, I made up a story like that . . . He was scribbling notes like mad."

"I was in there once, when I first got here," said DeWitt. "He asked me how come I was so depressed. I told him (whoosh inhale) it was cuz I didn't win the fucking lottery."

"Really." We rolled on. "DeWitt, where you going when you get out of here?" Long silence. Through the window in the passageway I could see the greathouse standing in the darkness ahead of us, yellow light streaming out of the ground floor windows, the upper floors dead and dark. Fanny pushed the gurney from behind. DeWitt rolled to my right, following us through every turn by sound.

"That's a question we don't ask around here much. Oh, you can ask Joel—he'll get a lot of money from the TA for his accident. But don't ask me, man, I don't know. I been here six months and I . . ."

We rolled through the swinging doors of the gym and were greeted by a burst of noise and color.

They parked me in the back of the gym, where the other horizontal patients were. "You okay here, Willie?"

"Sure. I dig drive-ins." They joined the other couples seated in wheel and folding chairs in the front half of the gym.

It was a pretty good movie too, in color, about jewel thieves. Warren Beatty or somebody was cutting through glass, swinging around ceilings, and in general wreaking hell with the insurance company that had underwritten some diamond exhibition.

About halfway through the movie, though, I started to cry—for these cripples here? for me? I don't know, but I cried through the whole second half of the movie, silently, and tears ran down my face and into my ears while Warren or somebody ran like a man with his ass afire through the streets and mosques of Istanbul.

8

Ulcers Aweigh

A lemon-yellow sun shone out of a powder-blue sky down upon a white ambulance that streaked along the almost deserted parkway, red light flashing despite the absence of traffic.

In the back of the ambulance, my mother and an attendant chatted amiably while I lay back, humming all the service songs I could think of, caissons rolling along through the halls of Montezuma, and all that. "The army takes care of its own." And its own's own. And so on? Junior Birdman First Class Willie Nasaw reporting for hospitalization, Suh!

Occasionally I would shiver, and my mother would hasten to throw a blanket over me, or I would sweat, and she would remove one. My crying jag had lasted most of the night—maybe it dehydrated me or something, but anyway, the fever was back, and I was feeling pretty strung out.

The traffic grew thicker at the George Washington Bridge, over which we had to pass—some foul-up at the tollbooth; but the cops waved us around the mess and through the toll plaza—I felt like a VIP.

The driver used the siren only once, in Manhattan at my insistence. "I don't mind," he said. "Everybody asks for it. Of course, I'm not supposed to, but . . ." Ahooga ahooga ahooga. Far out, a European-style sireen. It's the Gestapo coming for Anne Frank. Ahooga ahooga.

But before we reached Queens the shivering grew more intense, took over until *it* was shivering *me*, with my teeth going clicketyclicketyclick and my thighs twitching.

"Can't you give him anything?" my mother asked the attendant.

"We'll be there soon, ma'am," he answered.

Couldn't be too soon for me. I kind of drew into myself to wait it out and was dimly aware when we entered the hospital through a subsurface tunnel. Then things began to move at a rate to which I had grown unaccustomed up at FCRC.

Men and women in white clustered around me. "All right ma'am, we'll take good care of him," and before she could protest, my mother was allowed to kiss me good-bye and then steered away.

"Fever," I heard a shit-sure doctor voice say. I had closed my eyes to hide. "Urinary infection. Malnutrition. Decubitus ulcer, left heel. Drop foot, both feet. Jesus, he *came* from a hospital? Looks like a POW."

"How do you feel, kid?"

"Hot. Cold. I dunno."

"Right." Then he was gone, but his memory lingered on. I was jabbed in the left arm with an antibiotic and in the ass with the dope he had ordered.

And as they rolled me up to the neurology ward, I felt the warm golden tide roll in over my brain, and

I slept easy for the first time since I had left Farmington so long ago.

Inspection on Desolation Row

Monday morning, oh nine fifteen. Christ, we've only got forty-five minutes till inspection, and the ward is dissolved into a flurry of activity.

All the ambulatory patients, the ones whose beds are lined up along the eastern half of the ward, are up and working. Mopping the floors, dusting everything, straightening the beds—mine gets straightened two or three times a minute.

My half of the ward, the patients are all fixedly horizontal. "Desolation Row," we are called. We're straightening our bedside tables, combing our hair, giving each other directions.

"Okay, you got it now?" asks Slich, from the bed on my right. "You're a civilian, so you don't have to salute, so you just lie there at attention, hands at your sides . . ."

"Over or under the sheets?"

"Ummm. Under."

"Right."

"And don't speak to the Commander unless he speaks to you first. And if he asks if everything's all right, say yes sir! And if he asks if you have any complaints, say no sir! Only you're a civilian so you don't have to say sir. Only you better anyway."

"Gotcha, Slich . . . Hey, who's that over there?"

"Who?"

"That skinny guy over there falling asleep pushing the broom."

"Kennedy. We get him this week. They'll do some tests, say there's nothing wrong with him, send him down to Psychiatric, they keep him a week, send him up here for more tests."

"Battle fatigue?"

"As bad as you can get in Louisiana."

While we were talking, my bed got adjusted a few more times, and men kept stuffing things under my covers—magazines, candy bars, last minute discoveries. By oh nine five nine every man in Desolation Row, conscious or no, was lying a couple of inches higher than he had been at oh nine hundred.

The Commander was fifteen minutes late, preceded thrice by rumors of his imminent arrival. The last rumor was the kicker, though—bodies stiffened, and flop sweat ran in rivulets down freshly shaved faces. "A Captain."

Who? Which one? Not old soandso?

"No, a new one. Look sharp for chrissakes."

I couldn't see what all the fuss was about, personally. It was a hell of a show. The Captain looked like a nice enough man, not unlike Uncle Lou if you substituted a glittering white uniform for the rumpled blue suit.

But you couldn't see the Captain except for brief glimpses afforded by the shifting crowd he was in. Some crowd. Sisters and cousins whom he reckoned by the dozens. The Commander and a Lieutenant Commander and nurses all above the rank of Lieutenant, and an ensign whose job it was to hand the Captain the steel-jacketed charts of each patient.

The patients, except for me, were all active duty Marines or sailors, enlisted men and noncoms; almost all back from Nam. The Captain started down the other end of the ward, glancing at each man's chart, leaning in close for a question, sometimes making a notation. In between beds, he checked around for dirt, dust, or disorder.

At one point, when he was down at the far end of the ward, I felt my right arm jostled, lifted, and a pile of magazines shoved underneath. I looked around and saw a corpsman give me a wink. "Almost missed those," he whispered.

Then the entourage headed up Desolation Row, and I felt unaccountable feelings of guilt and fears of discovery mingled with a rush of stage fright. But when the Captain glanced at my chart, then looked up at me, his eyes were kind.

"Gave you quite a time in that other hospital, eh son?"

"Yessir."

"Civilians." Harumph. Then he did an unexpected thing. He stuck out his hand and said, "Welcome aboard."

And I did a stupid thing. I stuck out my hand from under the covers, and that parvenu stack of magazines tumbled out onto the floor. One at a time. Like silverware falling from Harpo's sleeve. Plop—Dude. Plop—Rogue, Stag, Cavalier . . .

The Captain looked down, waited for the parade to end, then shook my hand and leaned down to my ear. Said, "You'll make a sailor yet." Then on to the next bed as the corpsmen scrambled to pick up the magazines.

We passed the inspection.

Everybody agreed it was pretty goddam lucky I

was a civilian. I pretty goddam well agreed. Anyhow, nobody got mad at me, which was just as well, because I'd made some friends yesterday, and I didn't want to lose them already.

It was a good thing that yesterday, my first full day at the Naval Hospital, was a Sunday. Family day. Ever notice how much nicer everybody is when their family's around?

My family was there, too, in the person of my mother. And I had two surprise visitors.

I could hear them coming away down the ward. Rather I could hear the whistles and imagine the eyeball-popping that invariably accompanied any reasonably good-looking, reasonably young female with the misfortune to venture upon the ward.

It was Capt Rico's sister Therese. She was in no danger of assault, though, either physical or verbal, for she was accompanied by Rico's mother, Big Marie, and no *well* Marine, much less a sick one here, was going to tangle with *her*.

Big Marie brought with her a basket of assorted, wrapped goodies, and left me with explicit instructions to open only one each day. Therese left me somewhat higher in the respect of my comrades in arms. Seems like somehow they got the idea that this good-looking girl was *my* girl. Seems like somehow I let the impression stand.

Cheap Thrills

Monday night. Outside the ward windows, a cold summer rain fell from a starless sky. Cpl. Battaglia paced the ward floor nervously, dragging his braced left leg behind him, glancing up from time to time to the ward clock on the wall behind the nurses' station. Oh nine fifty, it said.

"He's got ten minutes."

"He'll make it, Jim. He always does," someone whistled in the dark.

"Who? What?" I asked. I was turned over on my stomach getting a shoulder rub.

"The Limey."

"Oh." I had seen the dark-haired Marine on the ward, with burning black eyes and a cockney accent, but was unsure if he was a patient or a corpsman. "Where is he?"

"Out getting drunk . . ." "Getting laid . . ." "In a fight . . ." "Fucking around . . ." came a chorus of voices from men I'd thought asleep or uninterested, but who were apparently watching the clock too. Battaglia hunched his broad shoulders in a who-knows gesture.

"Hard to tell. He gets a pass almost every night. Hard to say where he is now. But he's got ten—no, eight—minutes to make it back before they close the gates."

There were two minutes left when a short figure in civilian clothes rushed in the ward past my bed, and the tension in the room eased. Battaglia turned from his pacing and limped leisurely back to his bed as though the Limey's arrival had been the farthest thing from his mind.

Lt. (jg.) Gray discontinued my shoulder rub and stood up.

"That's everybody, then," she said. "Lights out in fifteen minutes." She returned to the dope deppo, the men could hold their pose of nonchalance no longer and broke out in a ragged chorus.

"What happened tonight?" "Who was she?" "Have a good time?" "Jesus, I didn't think you were gonna make it," they said, and then, in near unison, "Holy shit!" as the Limey turned to us from his bed in the far corner, even from halfway across the ward I could see a face that would have done Carmine Basilio proud.

The left eyebrow was split, and a mouse—no, a rat—was beginning to shine purple under the left eye. His upper lip was pulled into a sneer by a cut directly over the left eyetooth.

"Awright, awright, give a fella a minute to catch 'is bref, wi' ya? I'w tell ya, I alwize do, don' I?"

"Oh no, Stephen," said Nurse Gray, hurrying to his bed with a wet washcloth. "What happened this time?"

"I walked into a door."

"Don't pull that crap with me," she snapped back. "I've been patching you up for a month now, and I haven't reported you yet. Though how we're going to hide this one I don't know."

Then, as she ministered to his face, and as it began to look like hamburger painted with Mercurochrome, he acted out his evening's entertainment like an experienced monologist until the same vivid picture was painted in each of our minds.

It was unjust, that's what it was, unjust. I mean, there the Limey was, sitting in this bar around the corner, minding his own business, talking to this loose girl, when a hand grabbed him by the shoulder, spun him around, and caught him in the eye with a long looping right. He went down, came right up, laid the guy out with some karate, and took care of two of the guy's friends; then there was a short brawl, and the bouncers cleared out the place.

Out in the street, he met his attacker, who apologized—mistaken identity—and, arm in arm, they returned to the bar and bought each other drinks till closing. The girl?

"Oh, the twitch split."

As I waited for my Seconal to waft me off that night after lights out, I relived the Limey's adventure. I saw that punch coming, laid out those civilians myself, enjoyed the camaraderie, bought a round of drinks.

So, I imagine, did several other heads in the ward.

Some sort of symbiosis at work here, Inspector?

Possibly.

The Three K's

Wednesday afternoon. We've been invaded—overrun—our rear cut off—no possibility of retreat—vicious hand-to-hand fighting—ammunition gone—only our bayonets—and the enemy with an apparently limitless supply of Kool-Aid and cookies. I tell you, it was one tight squeeze.

Those Red Cross ladies are tough.

They prepare their own Kool-Aid in a 1:50 ratio. They bake their own cookies, black-bottom chocolate chip. And Slich, in the next bed, informed me I'd damn well better drink a whole cup and eat a cookie, or I'd hurt their feelings.

"It's sort of a responsibility," he said. "I recommend you drink it slow, though, or they'll refill it."

There were only three of them in embroidered red-

and-blue/gray-on-white striped smocks and ubiquitous red crosses; overpowered the whole ward.

Four, really, there was a mad old man with them, hawonking on a harmonica fiendishly, cheeks puffing, face red. He had a vast repertoire—all Stephen Foster tunes—and he danced behind the Kool-Aid cart like a demented leprechaun.

They fanned out through the ward to comfort us, and each wended her way over to me to make contact. They all managed to veil their disappointment at learning I was a dependent and not a war hero.

They weren't content just to dispense the three k's (that's Kool-Aid, kookies, and kindness, Kaptain) though. They also forced us to play games.

One, I remember, was a trivia game. They made up the questions though, and culled them, naturally enough, from their own experience. (Gawd, I shudder to think of the pivotal roles these biweekly sessions must have played in their own bleak lives.) So I moved my magnet marker farther faster than anybody in the ward, pulling ahead of the former champion, Sparky Geshlieder, by knowing two of the Lennon Sisters' names and identifying Alice Faye as Phil Harris' wife.

I clinched it with Elias Howe, and was duly rewarded with a bottle of donated Avon aftershave in a carriage-shaped bottle.

"Sorry to take advantage of you, Sparky," I told him when he wheeled to my bed to congratulate me. "I know you've been in the bush since nineteen-thirty —probably missed Alice's wedding."

"Shit, I don't even know what a sewing machine is," he said. "But don't worry about it. I already got three bottles like that."

"Three? Far out."

"Yeah. And two elephant bottles, one race car, and a horse."

"Trade you for an elephant."

"No chance."

Emission Impossible

I feel small and ugly, mean and hopeless. Dirty. Childish. Over a goddam picture in a magazine.

They're pretty easy here about lights out. If you can't sleep, they don't mind if you pull down the gooseneck lamp attached to the bed and read; or if you have a personal TV like some men, and an earplug, you can watch the Tonight show.

This night, I was excited in a new/old way around bedtime, and I could not for the life of me get to sleep.

Lt. Gray had been giving me a back rub—a partial massage really, since most of me was inaccessible beneath my cast. I lay on my stomach, and she kneaded the soft unused muscles of my shoulders and the slack flesh of my arms, and as she innocently rolled and lightly pummeled my numb buttocks and upper thighs, I, well, I got turned on. I don't think I had a hard-on, couldn't feel much down there, but behind my closed eyes, the two of us were in a bedroom, nude, and her ministrations were the prelude, or postlude, to some fancy fucking.

She finished, said good night, lights out, and I lay in the dark quivering, then turned on my lamp and pulled it down close to me, close enough so it made only a small spot of light in the dark. I thumbed through the pile of magazines that had remained mine since the debacle at inspection, until I found the picture that looked most like Nurse Gray: straight light-brown hair, clean features, lips moistened, parted, round-breasted, full-thighed. I replaced the airbrushed crotch, peeked beneath fig-leaf fingers to see nurse's sweet cunt, and stole a free hand down to my cock, flicked it lightly on the unfeeling flesh, then felt it engorge itself around the catheter.

One quick surge, one continuous motion in the flash of a second, hard-on, immediate glow of orgasm, blinding pain. That fucking catheter. Oh god, feels like my balls are going to explode. Then the come leaked from around the catheter, and I felt it warm on my fingers, and the worst part of the pain passed, to be replaced by a sharp ache.

Talk about negative reinforcement!

I threw all the magazines into the big round wastebasket between my bed and Slich's and turned out my light. I lay in the dark without sleeping. Feeling small. Ugly. Mean. Hopeless. Dirty. Childish.

9

PT Made Easy

I was, I'm afraid, rapidly becoming something of a nut-job on the subject of physical therapy.

This morning, for instance. My radar went whongg whongg whongg when two sailors entered the ward with a gurney. They were, I was sure, coming to take me to PT. Of course, I'd been sure for a week that any-one entering the ward with a uniform and an idle look was coming for me, but this time I was *sure* I was sure.

Needless to say, I was right this time, and by the time they had located me, all the blood had drained from my face and those muscles that I could control were shivering uncontrollably. Gave em quite a start, I did—they took my temperature and checked my blood pressure before they took me, for fear I'd somehow contracted malaria or some other exotic disease.

Speaking of exotic diseases! The delicious rumor making the rounds is that we have, as a fellow patient, a CPO's wife who was bitten by some indigenous rabid rodent in Malaysia and is suffering out the incurable terminal stages of rabies in an isolation room some-where in the bowels of the hospital. A few times a day, one of us will cut short all conversation with a "Listen! Hear that?" and we will all shudder together and mutually hallucinate lupine howls.

Late at night, too, alone and unaided, I imagine I can hear her howling, and envision her chained to a bed snarling and snapping.

As far as physical therapy went, though, this time reality was no match for my fiercest imaginings. They brought me into a screened-off cubicle, where I was joined by a young, curly-headed sailor named Tim—sparse mustache and big dimples exaggerated by an even bigger grin.

"Jesus," he said. "Unlax, will ya?" It was his theory that any PT who caused pain was a bullshitter, and he extended his theory into practice. He would hang one of my legs over the side of the gurney with a light weight around the ankle and let gravity do the work. That first day, I gained ten degrees of movement in my right leg and fifteen in my left, and he promised more, just as painlessly, our next session.

I was back to the ward in time for lunch, which was lucky, for I found my appetite returning, along with some semblance of health.

After lunch the Red Cross returned to consolidate its hold on the territory, but it was a whole different trip this time.

"This," Slich clued me, "is why we put up with that other shit."

"This" proved to be a good movie of recent vintage, donated for viewing in military hospitals by the studios, and, no doubt, personally selected and approved by Bob Hope. Of course, our good gray ladies managed to imbue the whole thing with a personal touch via the agency of some home-popped popcorn, shards of which remained embedded in my gums for a week thereafter.

And after the movie, after dinner, after visiting hours ended at eight, by keeping my ears open, I learned a little about war.

Battle Cry: Oops

Sometimes a week would go by without a mention of Nam, then *bam*, one night they'd all get this glazed look in their eyes, and I knew I could ask questions.

They no more held it against me, or thought less of me, for not having been there, than I did of them for not being in a car accident.

The first night they talked about it, the catalyst was a new man moved in a few beds down Desolation Row. Boswell. Josh Boswell. Half Irish, half Indian. (A hell of a combination, somebody said, if he drinks like an Irishman and holds it like an Indian.) He looked as if he'd once been fat, as if his cheeks had bulged like a squirrel in the fall, but now he was wasted from a month in a Japanese halfway hospital—a month, I gathered, not unlike my first, and his walnut-colored skin had a sickly cast and hung in folds over his bones.

"You in Nam?" he asked me.

"Nope."

"You didn't miss shit." That seemed to be the prevailing sentiment.

Then he told me his story. A short one:

A narrow trail in the jungle, preswept for mines. But a fool—not to speak ill of the dead—imagined he heard machine-gun fire and dove for cover in the foliage to the side of the trail, dove right smack on top of a mine. There was so little left of him, ran the popular joke, they brought him home in a Baggie instead of a body bag. He never even had time to call for a medic.

Which was just as well, since Josh was the medic, and hadn't even had time to turn around himself, having been struck, sudden-wise, by a fragment of mine/Which severed his spine/End of rhyme.

By the time Josh was finished with his story, the men had that faraway look I mentioned, and they were ready to reminisce.

Like Slich. Riding in a half-track that got hit by a shell and turned over. Broke his back.

Battaglia. An ambush in the jungle. Machine-gun bullets stitched his thigh. Never saw what hit him.

It was the goddamnedest thing. Story after story. Accidents. No malice. Nobody ever saw the little yellow man that got to him.

Mortar fragments. Mines. Booby traps. Stray bullets.

"I felt like I was in somebody else's accident," said a cadaverous sailor named Bellows who went down with his tiny ship on river patrol in the Mekong Delta. "I mean, shit, I joined the Navy cause I figured it was safer."

Bellows, Battaglia, Boswell, Slich. Accidents. No blame. No credit.

"Maybe we all got into somebody else's accident," I ventured. Each man thought about it for a minute. Put a pretty effective damper on the conversation.

One there was, though, who told no war stories that night, nor any other for all I knew, and if not me, who?—for he lay in the bed to my left.

A bed that made me think of a crib, for the side-rails were always up, and the bed itself was cranked high above the floor to be more convenient for the corpsmen and nurses.

Didn't matter to him what height the bed was. Not a bit. He never moved, nor spoke, nor heard, nor thought. Nor dreamed, most likely.

His frontal lobe was gone. Blown away by a shell fragment. His head, with a concave brow, reminded me of nothing so much as a partially deflated volleyball. It was shaven, and grisly stubble grew all over, even to a widow's peak swooping down to the incurvature.

I learned to sleep on my right side those nights, because on my left he lay in a fetal position, hands and feet drawn up like a puppy playing dead, nose taped and tubed, eyes open in a ghastly blue stare.

"They'll wait a week," Slich told me, "then send him to the VA hospital."

"Then what?" I asked.

"*Then what?*" He mocked me, a touch bitterly, I thought. "What happens to anybody in a VA hospital? He rots. If he's lucky he dies first, then rots—but he rots."

TILT!

I overheard a funny story on the way to physical therapy this morning.

They had me out in the hall on a gurney—I had my eyes half shut against the fluorescent lights hung from the ceiling—and there were two doctors nearby chatting. One, I deduced from the pin stuck in his lapel and from his grim demeanor, was a neurosurgeon. The other was reacting to something the brain man had said.

"Jesus, no, she left the guard off the drill?"

"Unh hunh."

"And you forgot to check?"

"Well, what the fuck, I'm supposed to double check every fucking thing?" A touch of anger.

The drill, I gathered, was being employed to remove a plug of bone from an enlisted man's skull, the better to remove a benign tumor that had affixed itself to the temporal lobe. The guard was to prevent the drill from biting too deeply through the skull to the brain.

"How far in did you slip?" asked the obviously horrified and fascinated (and obviously nonsurgical) other MD.

"Oh, a half-inch."

"What'd you . . . I mean . . . how . . . I mean. . ."

"What the hell," said the neurosurgeon. "So he lost a few memories. Enlisted men aren't supposed to think."

This whole morning in PT was something of an adventure. My first vertical adventure in some months. Well, almost vertical. Diagonal.

They removed the urine bottle, clipped the catheter off, and taped it to my leg. Then they transferred me to a tilt table and, to make a long story short, tilted me.

I remember feeling queasy, queasier, queasiest, as

they tipped me ten degrees clockwise every five minutes. That's head forward, up; feet downward, back. I'd been lying down so long that vertical memories were with me only in dreams. All strapped in now, tilt, a taste more, I felt as if I was going to slide off the board to the floor. Irrational fear. Dizzy. Fog. Black.

They tell me that at fifty-five degrees my eyes rolled back in my head and I passed out cold. I only remember coming to lying on my back, my ears ringing and the skin of my face tightened and prickly with pins and needles.

Tim looked down at me despairingly.

"Sorry about that, Willie. But you're supposed to tell us when it gets to be too much."

"How do I know what's too much?"

"Well, when it gets uncomfortable."

"Tim, I'm always uncomfortable."

Attempted Piss

One of the doctors was by again this morning. Told me most of the FCRC damage has been undone. The bedsore on my heel has scabbed over, and the bladder infection is down to acceptable levels.

Acceptable? For whom?

"Well, there's always going to be some infection with a foreign agent in the bladder."

Foreign agent! Exotic notions of spies danced through my brain.

"We're going to try to take out the catheter this afternoon."

Try? Is it stuck or something?

"No. I mean we're going to remove it and see if you can void without it."

Void! Aaah. The black holes of space. The nothingness in my bladder. The word had a ring to it.

Sure enough, after lunch (drink a lot of water so you have that with which to void) Lou the Corpsman visits me with a scissors and snips the catheter, which slides out of my prick like a dying garter snake.

I hardly know how to describe just how miserable a failure the experiment was. Wait! I know exactly how. Look at your forearm. Measure off halfway between elbow and wrist. Mark the spot. Now try to bend your arm there.

What do you mean how? Just bend it.

—I can't.

Try.

—I can't.

You used to be able to.

—It doesn't bend there.

Try.

—It hurts.

Try.

—I can't.

Bear down.

—Aaaaaah! Fuuuuck!

Get the picture? I lay there stupidly, looking at my groin, at my prick, trying to remember how I used to piss, but you know, I always used to take it for granted. I mean, when I had to piss, I pissed.

So now—nothing. I watch. The bladder fills and fills.

"I can't. I can't. Jesus, I'm gonna burst. Put the damn thing back in."

"Doctor said to wait an hour, Willie."

"Fuck you! Fuck you! Fuck you!"

After fifty-five minutes Lou replaced the catheter. The effect was rather like tapping a warm keg of beer with an ice pick. We both got soaked with warm, clear urine.

Lou cleaned us both up matter-of-factly, and I lay back in an exhausted mild depression for the rest of the afternoon.

I say mild depression. One thing I've been learning lately is a resistance to bad news.

I mean, shit, the other side of this bladder bit is Slich. His sphincter is slack where mine is spastic, so his piss flows easily. And uncontrollably. Which means his apparatus involves a condom around his prick, permanently, and a tube attached to the end of the condom, and a urine bag attached to the tube. *And that's it*. Forever.

Poor Slich. Lucky Willie.

Besides, I'm gonna get a surprise late this afternoon for my perseverance under fire.

Said surprise is to be a reward for my sterling performance yesterday in physical therapy.

And here it comes now.

A big old wooden wheelchair, an invalid chair, more properly, with a high slatted back, and long leg supports, old wooden-rimmed wheels.

It creaks as they position it by my bed, lock the wheels.

Then Lou grabs me under the shoulders, two nurses each take a leg, up and over, whoops a daisy, and I settle down into the chair, the back of which is tilted slightly to a forty-five-degree angle.

They comfort me with pillows, a lap robe, and a new *Sports Illustrated*.

"Hey," I ask, "can't I wheel myself?"

"Not with this kind of chair," says Lou. "One thing at a time."

Then he wheels me into the solarium at the end of the hall, sits me by a window. "You comfortable?"

"Yeah."

"Okay, be back in a half hour."

And here I sit. Ho hum.

It's your standard solarium. A few plants. A few leather chairs with the seats cracking. Old magazines strewn casually on Salvation Army end tables. A spectacular view of the hospital parking lot.

Still, in a way, it's a dream come true. For a month I have been daydreaming about sitting up, being out of bed. I never envisioned this odd angle they've got me parked at, nor the dependence on an aide to wheel me, but after all, here I am. I should be happy.

Within ten minutes I am bored out of my skull.

Within twenty minutes, tears of frustration are rolling silently down my cheeks.

Within twenty-five minutes every muscle in my body is screaming from the unaccustomed strain, and if my back had hands it would cut my throat.

After forty-five minutes, Lou returns. "I gave you some extra time," he tells me.

Thanks Lou. I have to wait another ten slow minutes before Lou can scout up sufficient manpower to lift me back in my bed.

My bed. It never felt so good.

I sleep the sleep of the just that evening, sleep right through my mother's visit, and am all slept out by bedtime—which means a wakeful night, eyes open in the dark, trying (fat fucking chance) not to think of the future.

Whatever the hell the future is. It's unclear, a series of old half-remembered images: cripples sitting in wheelchairs forlorn on the edges of crowds; cripples waiting plaintively at the edge of curbs; cripples tottering on steel crutches. I see myself in all those pictures, shudder, wish hard for sleep.

I dozed off a little before dawn, into one of those light sleeps where dreams take on a rational aspect, and awakened an hour before breakfast. I killed the time writing out the dream I'd had, a dream so real I can still see it. It was about gods. And (natch) cripples. I include it here for your delectation.

Vulcan

Vulcan, blacksmith of the gods, himself a god, was a cripple.

He was a simple, honest god, not bright, but reliable. He spent the greater part of eternity hard awork at his smithy, deep in the bowels of Olympus, in a cave, the mouth of which was perpetually hidden by black angry clouds that cloaked the daylight, consigning the smithy to darkness relieved only by the red fires of the forge.

And there, in the cavern, sweaty body and shiny black leather apron lit darkly by the flames, Vulcan was most happy. There were none to pity him there, none to cast sidelong glances at his massive hand-wrought silver leg brace or his heavy black-walnut staff with its burnished silver head and filigree work.

He loved the dark and the flames, the sweat and the

leather, the precious metal; and out of this love he would fashion weapons and armor for the gods, snuffboxes and jewelry too, for the gods were nothing if not vain. Thinking himself unhandsome, he worked no trinkets for himself, but instead, for the joy of it, at the end of each day he would design collages from the scrapes and drops of rare metal, and he would stud these constructs with gems—diamonds, sapphires, rubies—and line the walls of his cave, which came in time to be covered with the gleaming designs until the very cave winked back the firelight.

But Vulcan's simple heart was not fully at rest, his happiness was not complete. And one day, while he was drop-forging a hammer for Thor from Uru steel, a question came to his heretofore largely unquestioning mind. Straightaway he dropped his work and limped out of the cave and across the mountain to Great Jupiter's Throne.

"Vulcan, ol buddy ol friend, welcome," said Jupiter with a smile that lit the firmament." You must be tired. Pull up a cloud. Have a drink." And Vulcan sipped some ambrosia from a heavy gold cup he had with his own hands cast upon the occasion of Jupiter's ascension to the throne, and he rested his leg upon the godly purple satin cushion stuffed with hummingbird feathers, fetched at Jupiter's command.

"What's up?" asked Jupiter, when Vulcan was rested.

"Two questions," answered Vulcan.

"By all means," said Jupiter expansively, in his annoying manner.

"Why am I a cripple among the gods, and, can I not be a cripple?"

"Oh," said Jupiter. "That." And he hummed and

scratched and gnashed his teeth in thought. Vulcan waited patiently the while. After an eon or so, Jupiter raised his head.

"I didn't make you a cripple, as far as I can remember. I think the fact that you are crippled has to do with men; maybe they need a cripple god—you know, like they need a king god and a war god and all that other bullshit."

"Oh," said Vulcan, not quite understanding.

"As for the second question, I didn't make you, and I can't heal you. I got no experience, y' understand; I mean, you're the only cripple here.

"But I got an idea. There's lots of cripples among men, and a lot of men make a living claiming to be able to cure them. Maybe if you visited the earth as a mortal, they could help you. I recommend you go as an animal—men are kinder to their pets than they are to each other."

So it was that Vulcan came to earth as a humble dog.

A very humble dog. He found himself muddy, wet, smelly, bedraggled, limping on three legs down a rainy New York sidewalk.

"I don't see how this is going to help much," he thought to himself as snarling men kicked him into the gutter.

But he remembered Jupiter's instructions and hopped up the steps to a brownstone house upon the wall of which, beneath a white doorbell, hung a shingle with the inscription, Arthur Molesworth, DVM, Please Ring Bell.

But Vulcan couldn't reach the bell, so he lay on the steps and snoozed until he was rudely awakened when a woman in a white uniform tripped over him.

"Doctor," she called back into the house, "there's another stray on the doorstep."

"Shit," came a man's voice, and then the man himself appeared. "What do they think this is, the goddam ASPCA?" Unbidden, Vulcan arose and limped into the house.

"Oh well," said the doctor, "I might as well take a look."

"Oh Art," said the woman, "you're such a saint." The man chuckled and squeezed her ass, then followed Vulcan into the examining room and lifted him onto the table, where he poked and prodded.

"Complete hip displacement," said the doctor. "Nothing for it but to put him out of his misery."

"Thank you, O wise Jupiter," thought Vulcan, misunderstanding the euphemism and wagging his tail as he faded into unconsciousness upon the injection of the poison.

He awakened at Jupiter's throne, and, trying a step, found his limp unallayed in the least.

"I thought," he started to say, "I mean, you said . . . that is . . . I thought the man, the doctor said . . ." Then he caught himself and said, "It didn't work?"

"Ahhhh . . . Vulcan," said Jupiter, who had from his omniscient throne followed the lame god's misadventures among the mortals, "I was half right and half wrong. Men do have help for cripples, but apparently it doesn't work for gods."

"Why not?" asked Vulcan, staff in hand, readying himself for the long walk back to his smithy.

"Because," said Jupiter, "we are immortal."

Poor baby. Doesn't seem to matter how many or few my troubles are—I can still manage to work up a good pity party.

I mean, really now, doncha fall for that old hook, me whining about my troubles sitting up or pissing.

Because I'm well fed, three squares a day, and if I choose not to eat—well, it's the choice that matters.

The pain is pretty acceptable—I get Darvon, and, when I really hurt, a neat-o pill called Percodan. That's all right.

Lots of good care; they got corpsmen to spare here, and each corpsman has a personal stake in the care level, for each is serving six months here prefatory to going over to Nam to serve as a combat medic to the Marines. And most of them (not some—most) will end up here, or in a ward like it somewhere.

So you can bet your ass there's lots of love goes into the care.

Pretty nurses too. Well, two pretty nurses. They are all officers.

And movies.

It isn't utopia by any means. Which is to say it has no air conditioning (my cast was like a greenhouse in the summer heat) and I have no television.

But be of good hope, faithful. Utopia is coming. Really it is. Not far off, either.

Because it's not far as the crow flies from the Queens Naval Hospital to the great New Canaan Hospital complex in the Bronx.

By ambulance though, you have to ride toward the morning sun on the Cross-Island, and cross either the slick new gliding concrete Throgs Neck Bridge or the solid old Bronx Whitestone.

It's not a bad ride, after rush hour on a sunny summer's day, and now that you can sit up (a little) in the ambulance, you can see—in addition to the cotton candy clouds in the blue sky—a million suns reflected dancing in the water.

Swing low, sweet chariot, and carry me to hebben's do'.

Honorable Discharge

I knew after the first week I couldn't stay at the Naval Hospital after I was more or less healed—they had no facilities for rehabilitation. But I didn't know where I was going until Uncle Lou paid me another visit.

The subject was money, and the money was no object, he told me; the army had to pick up the bill for any hospital I went to, the sky was the limit, and all I had to do was pick my spot.

Seven come eleven it was falling my way at last. So I sent my mother out to reconnoiter and select a suitable base camp. She returned to me on the hottest day of the summer—tropical fungi were springing up full grown upon the inside of my cast, and the corpsmen were crossing from bed to bed bringing the temporary succor of alcohol sponge baths.

When my mother described New Canaan, visions of (what else?) milk and honey leaped to my fevered brow, and when she mentioned air conditioning, I fair began to salivate, a waste of precious bodily fluids in that humid New York heat.

"That's it," I said. "When can I leave?"

"And TV . . ."

"I told you, I like it, I'm ready. When? Today?"

Turned out I had to wait a day. Perversely, I rooted for the heat wave to continue, to sweeten the move even more.

So it was that, when the next morning dawned hot as a Mexican sheep dog, I reveled secretly in the heat. Reveled because it was to be my last day in the furnace; reveled secretly because, after all, it would be a long time before my friends would receive any climatic relief.

For, by the idiosyncrasies of governmental legislation, dependents of World War II vets could luxuriate in whatever surroundings they chose, while the heroes of Vietnam, when readied by the fine service hospitals for rehabilitation, would be abandoned to the limbo of the Veterans Administration Hospitals, there, for the most part, to lie untended in their own filth until— the end?

It was one of those things we didn't talk about much.

Anyhow, the morning of my departure, they cleaned me up, scrubbed me down, switched me to a portable urine bag, packed up my charts, and rolled me down to the vehicle tunnel to await an ambulance.

Everyone bid me a fond, proper good-bye, but without much attachment, for they knew, as I did, that my place would be taken soon enough by another young man with a ruined body, whom they would repair and care for until he was well enough to be shipped to VA oblivion.

10

Introduction to Rehabilitation

Often, in the Ryder Rehabilitation Center of New Canaan Hospital, when people would ask me how the rehabilitation was going, I'd tell them a little parable. Eventually I typed it out on the brand spanking new electric machine in Occupational Therapy. Not during my regular session, of course; that was taken up by my usual game of cribbage.

Here's the parable. I call it:

The Rehabilitation of Cripple Jake

It was in that time between B.C. and A.D. that Jake, illegitimate offspring of a fleeting night's passion shared by an otherwise respectable dark-eyed Jewish maiden and a handsome, flashing, but undeniably goyish Roman soldier, lived. So unwelcome was the event of his birth that Jake and his mama were thrown the hell out of his grandfather's house, she to die within five years from a combination of shame and pneumonia, he to become one of the greatest of Jerusalem's street rat beggars and thieves. He was supple, daring, resourceful, but

111

flawed by the greed and pride that were to prove his undoing.

For, at age thirteen, he determined to find his grandfather and claim what he felt was his birthright. Once found, the grandfather, a prime, hearty man of sixty, hardened by forty years as a stonemason, kicked him the hell out of the house again, quite literally. The resulting fall, down six hand-built stone steps, broke Jake's spine and left him, as the saying goes, a hopeless cripple.

Well, not hopeless; his grandfather, in remorse, took him in until his life was no longer in danger, bought him a fine low-wheeled cart, and *then* kicked him the hell out of the house, figuratively this time.

Now, being a paraplegic was not that much of a handicap in the begging game, if you could stay alive. So for the next few years Jake, known now as Cripple Jake, porgied his way around the hills of Jerusalem, his alms account at the local bank growing, his health rapidly deteriorating. He had decubitus ulcers from his ass to his heels, his urinary tract was broken down from bladder to kidneys, and he was in constant pain.

By the time he heard of a fabulous healer/messiah come to Jerusalem, the h/m had already been busted, and, word being that the fix was in, Cripple Jake figured he had no chance to get himself healed. Eventually, though, after the verdict, the grapevine published the route of the crucifixion, and Jake determined to get a good seat along the line of march that Friday.

Soon enough, Christ came trudging up the hill with his burden, and Cripple Jake scooted himself into the road. Before the guard could kick him out of the way, he had grabbed Jesus' ankle with a death grip and howled his plea to the Christ. The Son of Man, with a backhand gesture, loosed waves of force that knocked Jake off his cart.

When the cobwebs cleared, Christ was ten yards up the hill, and Cripple Jake, taking inventory while lying on the cobblestones, found his sores healed, his kidneys no longer throbbing, the pain in his legs . . . gone? Gone! He tried to scramble to his feet, but his legs failed him, and he fell on his ass.

"Jesus Christ," he screamed, "I'm still a cripple."

"Whadda ya want," Christ replied over his shoulder, "a miracle?"

The inspiration for that story came from what Dr. Hassel said to me my first afternoon, by way of fair warning and conversation while she stuck me with a pin (Sharp? Dull? Sharp? Dull?) and asked embarrassing personal questions. (Bowel movement? Any erections?)

What she said, more or less, was that they didn't perform any miracles there; that no one could regenerate dead nerve tissue; that I would have to make do the best I could with what I had; that I could work as much as I wanted to, as fast as I wanted to; and that if I worked very hard, I could be out of there by Christmas.

It was then August thirteenth, my dead father's birthday. I thought of him as I sank back into the most fantastic hospital bed I had ever been in, sighed, and turned on the TV suspended from the ceiling.

The Magic Button

Lemme see, now, where shall I begin to describe New Canaan? Got to do this right, y'know—it's to be our new home for quite awhile, as long as the other three hospitals combined.

I guess there were two things that got me off most that first day: one was the magic button and the other was the influx of visitors.

The Magic Button. A small console, really. I could, with this gadget the size of a transistor radio: turn the TV on and off, select channels, adjust volume, enjoy the same set of options with AM/FM radio, adjust the height of my bed and the tilt of the head, middle and foot, call the nurses, and with the flip of a roger-wilco over and out button speak to and hear them. Far out, eh?

The Visitors. They flowed in and out that first day like a spastic tide, most of them eager to see, as one put it, the first new patient under sixty-five we've had in a month. An exaggeration, but not by much. Mostly they'd catch me in between Magic Button experiments, introduce themselves, say: You must be tired, and split. I'll just run em by you the way they ran by me, and we'll sort em out later.

The nurses were uniformly nice: tall cool blond O'Hara; Novac, who looked like a Russian female shot-putter; Taliaferro, with a don't-shit-me attitude. They were the three RN's—too busy for a chat that day, but they all said howdy.

Then there were the aides, all black: sexy sullen Susan from Jamaica; Clark, whose arms hung to his knees—he was studying to be a psychiatric aide, which was more dangerous but paid better; Thomas, gentle, soft-handed, hair conked and parted on the right side arbitrarily.

And the therapists dropped in too. Lee, from PT,

already assigned to work with me, looked like a giant seen through the wrong end of a telescope, had a big black Zapata mustache; he reiterated Dr. Hassel's sentiments—I could work as much and as hard as I wanted to. I spent the longest time with the Occupational Therapist, Miss Kelly, Joan. She dropped in to say hi, admitted there wasn't too much her department could do for me, invited me in to use the facilities when I was up for it, and asked me if I played cards.

"Some," I said.

"Cribbage?"

"I've heard of the game."

"Want to learn?"

"Sure—penny a point, quarter a game, double for skunks, triple for double skunks."

"My," she said dryly, "you catch on fast."

So she left, returned with a board and a sealed pack of cards, and we chatted and laid a game.

I learned that she wasn't Irish, despite her name and button nose, but Jewish. She learned some fundamental weakness in my cribbage game that I've never been able to spot. Within a half hour, I was down, on paper anyway, two bucks, and was grateful for the chance to end the game supplied by the arrival of a man in a wheelchair.

He was a black man, and even seated he seemed very tall. She introduced him as Dr. Woodson, my fellow patient, a recent paraplegic. We nodded, shook hands, and he was gone. She left too.

I lay back exhausted but not at all unhappy, listened to the quiet hum of the air conditioning, delighted with this new karma that was going to be mine to work out and sure beyond a doubt that I wasn't going to be able to remember any of the names I had learned today. Which was all right—I would have plenty of time to learn them.

The Famous Cripples Series

I've just had the most fantastic idea.

What I've done is, I've envisioned a series of bubble gum cards: The Famous Cripples Series No. 1 through No. Whatever.

And with an eye to the practical, for a change, I've taken the idea further. The possibilities for merchandising are unbounded. Like I say, we start with bubble gum cards, work out a deal with the Topps Organization (trade you two Roy Campanellas for a Douglas Bader). Then maybe a Famous Cripples Series of medallions, by Norman Rockwell for the Franklin Mint. From there, the sky's the limit: Golden Books, Klassix Komix, TV, Movies, Fast Food Franchises.

Don't look at me that way. It's a far out idea. I even got a theme:

"Cripples! Lord love em. Every one of them got it so that the law of averages might spare us." Or maybe, "Everyone of *us* got it so that the law of averages might spare *you*."

Think about it, call me in the morning with your answer.

What the Plaster Saw

I seem to have this habit of describing people by their race, handicap (if any) and/or occupation. Is that bad?

Yeah, well, fuck it. I met the orthopedic doctor up in the cast room for the first time. He was Latin, and his handicap (if any) was that he couldn't speak English for shit.

I didn't even know he was the doctor—with his broken English, rumpled lab coat, canvas shoes, and generally cheerful demeanor, he was a ringer for an attendant or possibly an immigrant intern.

But no, he was the doctor, as I discovered when his first intelligible words were a request to the real cast room attendant (who had horn-rimmed glasses and Harvard med bearing) for a hundred and fifty cc's of Demerol.

Now that's a lot, particularly considering as how I wasn't in any pain, and that all they were gonna do (Nurse Novac had assured me as she wrestled me over to the gurney) was remove my cast to take some X-rays and measure me for a brace.

Doctor Corraldi looked down at me, dark eyes flashing with amusement as I protested, and pretended not to understand me.

"Hey, c'mon now," I said, not sure *why* they were giving me the dope, and twisted my arm away from the attendant, whereupon Corraldi informed me, cheerfully enough, that he was da doctor, and to let him know when I felt good. Then he shot me like a professional gunslinger—I never even saw his hand move.

Nawsuh, no mo' complaints mistah doctah suh, you jus' gives us niggers our dope, and you kin do wat you wants wif us.

I nodded out to the pleasant whine of the plaster saw (vibrates, no cut, he demonstrated on his own arm). Then a few zip-zips with the ole measuring tape, a few criss-crosses with adhesive tape to hold the now halved cast together, and me and my gurney were traveling back to the rehab ward.

Only I was stoned out of my head and slept through the afternoon.

Said Nurse Novac, lifting me singlehanded back to bed, upon observing my pinpoint pupils, "Oh that Corraldi!"

"He do this often?" I mumbled.

"Yes," she said. "I think it's a compensation because he feels uncomfortable about not speaking English."

"S'okay," I managed. "He speaks *my* language."

See, See Ryder ·

What with the bulky cast extending from collarbone to pelvis and restraining me from sitting fully upright, I couldn't fit into a regular wheelchair, but somewhere O'Hara found an old-style invalid's chair, slanted it back a bit, and wheeled me, half sitting, half reclining, around my new home.

The Ryder Rehabilitation Center wing of the New Canaan Medical Center lay in the shape of a square dumbbell behind New Canaan's main building.

The north square of the dumbbell was the residential section. Indirectly lighted rectangular rooms on three sides, the nurses' station on the fourth. And from the nurses' station stretched a long corridor to the south, which opened up into the square of the therapy/outpatient clinic, with gym, occupational therapy, hydrotherapy, and waiting room. As in the residents' wing, everything was pastel, indirectly lighted, wheelchair level, chrome-railed, and stainless.

Welcome to the 1980 World's Fair Bronx Expo, GE's Wonderful World of Cripples Pavilion, we hope you'll enjoy your stay.

But where are the people?

"It's Saturday. No therapy today. But just wait till Monday, the joint'll really be jumping."

"I can hardly wait."

My patience was scarcely improved when I returned to my room to find they'd moved a roommate in on me.

Morris. Old Morris.

I like to shit mah britches.

Wide World of Diabetes

If I was you, and I was getting on in years, I would pay awful close attention to my blood sugar count. I'd have it checked about twice a week. And if it started rising and I heard the word diabetes tossed around in my presence, I'd tell the doctor I was having trouble sleeping. Then he'd give me a prescription that I'd take to the druggist and the druggist would give me a bottle of little yellow or red pills, and I'd go someplace quiet and wash down the whole bottle with a pint of Old Overholt.

And hope for better luck next time around.

Which is what Morris should have done.

"Say hello to Morris," said O'Hara, returning me to my room after my tour.

"Hello, Morris," I said. He looked in my general direction with red, rheumy eyes, but he didn't quite understand, just nodded amiably at the sound of his name and lay back in bed. That was our contact for the afternoon.

I turned on the TV and watched Wide World of Sports—a passable way to spend a Saturday afternoon if you're paralyzed. They had two new ways to crash up cars, competitively, and the World Wrist-Wrestling Championship Semifinal Elimination live on tape from Petaluma, California. Good show. Didn't notice Morris again till dinner time.

He was flailing about with his mashed potatoes and mumbling loudly. I asked him whether he wanted a nurse; he flailed and mumbled, so I called one anyway, and an aide was dispatched to feed him and mop him up. It was while she was changing him that I noticed that his left leg ended at mid thigh in a neat stump.

I was pretty well inured to stumps by that time, so it didn't affect my appetite (which was remarkably poor anyway) in the least.

"How'd he lose that?" I asked Susan.

"Diabetes." She grinned and flashed a set of lovely white teeth.

"Hunh?"

And she explained how old diabetics often lost, in addition to their eyesight, their lower limbs, due to poor circulation and low resistance to infection. A random bruise might well become gangrenous, and then—whoops—amputation was next.

Personally, I can think of better ways to go.

We paid each other little attention that Saturday night. I watched TV, had a game of cribbage with Dr. Woodson (he skunked me; maybe I'm not as good as I thought), and sort of generally hung out till it was time for my Seconal, Mandelamine, ascorbic acid, and Darvon, and said good-bye to this plane until, I thought, Sunday morning.

I was awakened to the darkness by an old voice's mumbling, and I thought for one bad moment that I was back in Farmington ICU.

As my eyes adjusted to the dark, I saw Morris sitting up across the room, tears brimming out of his almost blind eyes, rolling down his old cheeks. He was shaking his head.

"I'm an old man, and I piss myself like a baby. Old man like a baby. I piss myself like a baby."

I felt like an interloper and tried inconspicuously to ring for a nurse. My stealth was sort of irrational, I suppose—I don't think he could see me.

The night nurse came down to change Morris—she bustled around and clucked soothingly at him, told me I could have another sleeping pill in a half hour, and delivered it accordingly.

Until it came, and for a short time thereafter, until it put me out, I lay in the dark and thought bitter thoughts about old men, and death, and me.

The next morning, Sunday, dawned dismal enough for me, although outside my room the sun shone brightly on the Bronx.

It was the kind of day that came to me, if not rarely, then infrequently. It wasn't so much how I felt as how the world felt to me.

Well, let me tell you what I did:

Nothing.

I refused all my pills except pain pills (and of those I requested more), I ate nothing, I drank not a drop of water. I didn't get hungry and I didn't get thirsty and I didn't get bored.

Let me tell you what I thought:

Nothing much.

I sort of wondered a whole lot of why's and why-me's, and sort of wished I was dead, but without any great passion.

Let me tell you what the staff did:

Nothing.

They left me alone and waited for my black fit to pass.

Let me tell you how it passed:

Naturally.

With the passing of the day.

Sure, black days hit me now and again. They were no more my fault than anybody else's, and no more to my debit than good days were to my credit.

But be still, Willie, you're no philosopher, and tomorrow is Monday. You've got work to do.

11

Workday

Lee's round brown eyes were lit up; his mouth opened and closed under the big black mustache, and he punched one big fist into the other palm, did a quarter pirouette one way then the other. He was trying to make a point.

"You are so fucking lucky. You . . . are so . . . lucky. You're gonna walk, man—You are going to . . . walk!"

"Maybe," I said. I was still in the afterblow of yesterday's blues.

"No maybe. Definitely. I can guarantee it."

"Oh come on."

"No, no." It was funny to see the muscle-bound therapist bóuncing up and down on his tiptoes. "For sure. Look, see these big muscles here, go down the front of the thighs?"

I allowed as how I did. He tapped mine.

"Flex that."

I did.

"Now the other one."

I did.

"That's *it*, man, that's the quadriceps. That's *all*

you need to walk, man. Even if you didn't have *any*
other muscles—and you do—you could still lift each
leg up and put it down.

"How good? I dunno. But you're not stuck in a
wheelchair. Maybe you'll have to use one for long
distances. Probably crutches, definitely braces—but
you'll walk."

A little of his enthusiasm began to seep into me.
I flicked the nose of my rubber vulture, which, with
my guitar and paraphernalia, my mother had brought
to me. "But right now I can't hardly even sit up."

"One step at a time. You can work like Doctor
Woodson does. Here's the deal I made with him—you're
only scheduled for two sessions a day, but I guarantee,
as long as you're down there, you'll have work to do.
As much as Doctor Hassel lets you do, anyway."

"Hassel?"

"The lady doctor. Didn't you meet her?"

"Oh yeah, she was the first one I saw."

"Yeah. She's your physiatrist—rehabilitation doctor. She's in charge. Well, really, you're in charge. No
shit. Just make noise. And work. Our only job is to get
you to work, so if you work, you're the boss."

"When do we start?"

"Now?"

"Outasite."

"C'mon." He trotted out flat-footed to find a gurney,
transferred me with my help, and we zipped down the
corridor at a dizzying rate. "I'll bring him back for
lunch, Nancy," he told Nurse Taliaferro.

"Keep him as long as you want," she said. "We
won't miss him. He was pretty depressing yesterday."
But she made it all right with a smile.

By eleven, though, I was more than ready to get back to my room. I'd learned five different ways to lift first three- then five-pound weights while lying on my back, and I'd repeated them, in series of ten, over and over, until I was soaked and the weights were slippery with sweat.

Then, just before I dropped the weights to the floor in surrender, Lee was at my side, taking them out of my hands and giving me a drink of water.

"You might as well drink it," he said, "or I'll pour it down your throat. You can't work if you're up in surgery getting bladder stones removed. Drink!"

Made sense. I did.

"Ready to go back?"

I nodded.

"Just a second. Let me take care of Morris." He went over to Morris, sitting in a wheelchair at the other side of the gym, dressed in T-shirt and shorts, idly raising and lowering a one-pound weight with his right hand and occasionally jerking his stump around like a flipper. Lee yelled into his ear, and Morris nodded his bald head and switched the weight to the other side.

Lee returned and began pushing my gurney back to the inpatient wing. "He's really working hard," he said about Morris. "I only hope we can get him walking before he dies."

I laughed. He looked down at me puzzled, then laughed himself. "Okay," he said, parking me by my bed. "You can transfer yourself. I'll just help with the bottle."

I could, and did.

"Come on back at one," he said. "I guarantee you some more work. Enjoy your lunch."

"Why Are You Reporting the Rape Now, Thirty Years Later?" "I Just Now Felt Like Talking About It."

"I am not a homo sex yew all. I am a sexual being." How many times you heard that bullshit line? Mostly from fags and dykes.

Oh Willie, don't be bitter. Don't resort to name-calling. I mean really, how can you feel used when, after all, you were the only one who got to come? And, as I recall, Willie old boy, you could have said stop at any time. Did you? (No.) Did you? (No.) Did you? Say anything? Except for a little shadowy groan there somewhere between the desire (his) and the spasm (yours).

Hey friend, I got you hooked? Practically salivating? About time we got a little goddam sex into this thing. Wha happen?

Well, Dr. Kinsey, it was late, quite late, of a midweek night, and I was experiencing some dis-comfort, not to mention pain. Pain? I *told* you not to mention pain. (Oh shit, I must be shook, doing old Soupy Sales routines.) In my nether regions. And no wonder. Upon cursory examination it was discovered that my catheter was blocked, possibly by an errant clump of mucus, and my bladder was filling.

Bad news. But no sweat. Just gotta change it. Hospital rules, though—oh the delicious irony—forbid the changing of male/female catheters except by males/females. So they asked Urogenital for the loan of Perry, a male nurse.

Now, putting Perry on the U-G floor was like leaving Superfly to guard the coke. I mean, not to be guilty of any rampaging stereotypes, but there was *no way*

Perry wasn't gay, this slim black man with processed, hennaed hair, who swished like a horse's tail in fly time. But still, you know, I'm a liberal, ahem, we're all liberals around here, and what I mean to say, if a man's . . . aaah . . . predilections, appetites, don't interfere with the performance of his duties . . .

So we howdied, and I lay back, daydreaming (of all things) of the tree-lined street where we used to play catchaflyisup. Perry busied himself down below, with a snip of the old catheter, which snaked out blindly with the release of the sterile saline solution that filled the little balloon that kept the catheter trapped in the bladder.

Then it was time, as always, for a little rubadubdub, got to kill those nasty germs before we put the new size sixteen red rubber Foley catheter in.

But the rubadubdub (I couldn't feel too good down there, on the outside of my skin) seemed to be taking a little longer than usual this time, and when I glanced down I saw Perry rubadubdubbing—what? Me, I guess, but I couldn't see *me*, the cast was in the way. I could only see Perry. He had his eyes half closed, his teeth bared a little, he was lost somewhere inside himself, and then swoop, he bent his head down and *now* I could see it. The stiff top end of my cock, gobbled in an instant into the end of his mouth. I couldn't feel anything (the sensation might come back, though, sometime, the doctors had said) but my cock was evidently enjoying things.

Still and all . . . I mean . . . what the hell? I cleared my throat (to speak? to protest?) but what came out was a pinched noise (half protest, half passion?), and Perry took his mouth off me, looked up.

And at that precise second, pop! I came, splawhoosh, into his upturned face. Then, for a frozen moment he watched me, and I watched the come dribble in gobs off his face.

And me? I couldn't split, captive in my own bed, so I copped out as best I could, closed my eyes, and lay back on the pillow, withdrew my presence.

So I don't know, I assume Perry mopped us both up, recathed me, and left.

But I have this awful feeling he thinks I engineered the whole thing, enjoyed it, and gushed in his eye for spite.

Not me, Perry. Honest.

A Seven-Letter Word for Nothing Left to Lose

Far out. Incredible. No words for it. Far out. I'm free. (Freedom is a relative thing.)

Once more around the hall. Shove the rim of the wheelchair wheels forward with a throwing motion. Zip. Zip, zip, zip, zip, and you've reached a full rate of speed by the corner of the hall, then grab the rail at full tilt and let your momentum throw you through the curve.

Wide World of Sports my ass. It's the wheelchair derby. Once more around the track here, then I'll, hmmm, let me see, I'll go out into the garden. That's . . . down the corridor here? No, that's speech therapy . . . ah yes, right through this door.

Hello tree. Hello sun. What? Low already. Good grief, time sure flies when your're having fun.

Of course I haven't always been this mobile. About five hours. But I've already forgotten what it felt like to be trapped in one place, unable to move without help.

No sir. It's a whole other ball game now.

Just a few minor things had to happen.

First thing that happened, at one, before I got down to PT, Lee and Dr. Hassel, Dr. Corraldi and a nurse all showed up in my room. With a big grin, Corraldi opened up my cast like a giant oyster. Then the nurse sponged off the layers of dead gray skin that had been sloughing off for the last few months and polished up my ribs which were showing through the transparent white skin.

Then . . . Ta Taa! The back brace. A leather and aluminum affair that strapped around my waist, using the pelvic bone, lower spine, and collarbone as pressure points to keep me sitting straight and take some of the weight off my spine.

They all smiled, admired the fit, wished me well, then split. Lee returned with a box and a wheelchair.

In the box was a leg bag. He showed me how to switch the catheter from the bottle to the new leg bag which fit under my pajama pants. Almost ready.

Then he demonstrated how to get from bed to chair. Pretty simple, really.

"Okay, first you have to get the bed to the height of the chair. Right. Then take out the arm of the chair, lay it aside. Make sure the wheels are locked. Always lock the wheels. Slide the removable leg/foot-rests of the chair away to the side—just push this button here with your thumb. Right.

"Now, grab the far arm of the chair with that hand, push up with your other hand to get the weight off your ass. Now! Slide! Don't worry about your legs. They'll follow. They have to, they're attached.

129

"Right. That's it. Let's practice a couple more times . . ."

Once he let me forget to lock the chair's wheels, and caught me as the chair rolled away and I headed for the floor. Just as sort of an extra lesson about locking the wheels.

"Okay, you're nearly set."

"Nearly? I can do it perfect."

"Sure. All you gotta do now is learn how to open doors."

Easier still. Nothing to it if the door opens out. Just throw it . . . whoops, I shoot backward (for every action there is an equal etc.). First lock the wheels, then throw the door forward, catch it before it recloses, unlock, scoot on through.

Slightly harder if the door opens toward you. You have to park at a forty-five degree angle to it, lock the wheels, pull it toward you, catch it behind you, unlock, scoot on through.

That is all ye know on earth and all ye need to know: how to get in and out of your wheelchair and how to open doors.

Anyway, that's all you need to know here at New Canaan where there are neither curbs nor stairs, where all is ramped and railed and wheelchair level.

But Jesus Fuck! It's a start.

Where shall I go now? Hmmm . . . think I'll try the patients' lounge.

Sittin and Chinnin

So I sit in my wheelchair in the little courtyard between the two wings of Ryder Rehab, sharing a joint

130

and chat with Dr. Woodson. It is a soft summer night, and above us stars shine in a sky of periwinkle at the horizon darkening to midnight blue at our zenith.

It is the good doctor's dope. He laughed at my surprise upon finding out that he smoked. "You young white kids think you invented it." Turns out they start smoking dope young in East St. Louis, where he grew up. "As a matter of fact, I almost lost interest in the stuff when all you started using it. Took some of the fun out."

He speaks in a soft voice with only gentle traces of black rhythms. "I had to learn to talk this way in medical school," he tells me.

We traded our usual "How did it happen?" stories—he laughing and shaking his great head in amusement when I described Capt Rico and the great oh zee switch; me listening wide-eyed to his story of flipping his Porsche on Third Avenue down around Nineteenth Street in Manhattan.

"The top was down, and I was thrown clear. I landed on my back on the sidewalk, and I knew what had happened right away."

He really meant he *knew*. He'd already made a diagnosis and prognosis before the ambulance arrived.

So. Here we sit. And smoke and chat in the mild summer air. He has a few advantages here, being a member of the staff (on sick leave, of course). He'll make arrangements for me to switch rooms and become his roommate as soon as possible.

He hands me a beddy-bye joint, and we roll inside and back to our rooms.

You know, life seems kind of sweet at the moment. I guess it all depends on where you're coming from.

Willie's Inferno

No one ever asked me how I would fill the inner circles of hell, upon whom I would inflict gaping chancres, whose flesh I would have fall from whose bones in front of whose wakeful eyes, whom I would have hold whose own entrails in whose very own hands, upon whom I would put the tortures of the damned. But if I were ever asked to draw up a blanket indictment on some group, I would, with only slight trepidation, finger the social workers.

I mean, one or two social workers were wonderful people, but like they say, you lie down with dogs you come up with fleas—I might not hesitate to burn the innocent if it would guarantee me the guilty. One guilty in particular.

Take this beauty sitting at my bedside. Please.

You gotta understand I got a pretty good deal worked out here, now that me and Dr. Woodson (I never called him anything else) are roomies. Since therapy doesn't start till ten, ten thirty, we order cold breakfasts—juice, cereal, fruit—which await our pleasure at our bedsides, and sleep it out until nine thirty or ten.

Like Lee said, if you're working, you write your own ticket here.

Which is why I'm so surprised to be awakened by a tap on the arm when my watch (set out so I can read it just by opening my eyes) only says eight forty-five. Jesus! And I stayed up for the whole "Tonight Show" last night.

I'm a little surprised too, to see this girl sitting at my bedside, her face (nice enough face) no more'n two, three feet from me. I regard her with one half-opened eye.

Straight brown hair pulled back, secured by a white stretch elastic headband, a beige jumper over a blouse with a Peter Pan collar. Does her mother dress her? What bothers me most, though, is the clipboard and the purple Flair pen.

"Are you Jonathan Nasaw?" she asks. I can see she's looking at my hospital wristlet (doubles as a body tag) so dissembling would be futile. (Unless I can convince her there's been a Prince and Pauper switch? Naah.)

I nod.

"Hello Jonathan. I'm Joan Parkinson." That must be the first line on the questionnaire she's got—Hello blank, I'm blank.

You've probably guessed she's a social worker. And she'd like to ask me a few questions.

I look over at Dr. Woodson, but he's asleep (or faking it pretty well). And I can't reach for my call button inconspicuously. Anyway, the nurses probably told her to come on down. So we start to play the game.

You can dig that answering questions about what's wrong with me for somebody who's obviously never had anything wrong with them does not exactly rank up there with brown paper packages tied up with string on my list of favorite things.

—Where was the accident?

This road that goes to this cemetery.

—What kind of car?

A red car.

—What was my state of mind at the time of the crippling accident?

The what?

—The uh accident.

I was okay.

—Was I feeling suicidal?

No more'n usual.

—What is my state of mind now?

I'm okay.

I mean, obviously, I figured if I was cool she'd go away, but she just had more and more questions, and I was getting more and more depressed, reliving that crap in detail, and when she turned the page over on her clipboard, and started in on a second page of embarrassing questions—I grew desperate. She made me feel, I dunno, like a cripple I guess. I thought I could read pity in her eyes, and that was something I'd been shielded from so far.

I looked across the room to Dr. Woodson (we faced each other in the roomy room, feet to feet) and sure nuff he was awake, watching the whole thing, grinning like a goddam Cheshire cat. I waggled an eyebrow, he grinned even more and clutched his throat.

"Hunh. Ha-waah. Huh huh hunkahunk a hunk. Hawaa."

The huge black man was obviously choking to death right before the girl's horrified eyes. Keerist, they didn't tell her about this in social worker's school.

"Haw, ch, ch . . . Hawhunh. Hunh."

We had to move fast. I rang for the nurse, reached around in my drawer, came up with . . . a roll of dental floss. I handed it to her.

"Quick," I said. "Give this to him. Hurry." She did. "Now wait outside." She left.

"Hunh hoo hoo, wha wha wha . . ." The doctor

kept it up until a nurse arrived, at which time we both dissolved into fits of laughter. I explained my problem, and Tough Titty Taliaferro (pronounced Tolliver, of course) agreed to rid me of my incubus.

"Thanks, doctor," I said.

"It was time to get up anyway," he managed between guffaws.

After all, what are friends for?

Goin Fwimmin

Good morning? A new blue and yellow nylon boxer type horizontal competition stripe bathing suit has appeared at the foot of my bed.

What the hell?

Twenty minutes pass, question answered, by Lee, who comes in wearing a bathrobe over a too small bathing suit.

"Painted you orange, you'd look just like the Thing."

"It's clobberin' time," he responded. "Got your suit on?"

"I'm working on it. Shouldn't take more'n half an hour."

"Take your time. Got anything to read?"

"Yeah. Or you could smoke a joint while you wait." Before I could show him where my stash was, he took a number out of his bathrobe pocket. "It probably would have got wet anyhow." He made no move to help me dress, properly enough, since he wasn't going to be able to follow me around and dress me the rest of my life.

I used one of the gadgets Joan from OT had given

me, a stick with a coat hook on the end, to drop the suit over my feet, then pull it up. It took twenty minutes to get ready, what with time out for tokes and stoned fumbling, but we had fun in the meantime.

"I don't want to get pushy," I said at one point, "but why are we wearing bathing suits?"

"You're going to stand up today, maybe walk," he answered.

"Oh. That explains it. No wonder I couldn't walk before. I didn't have a bathing suit on." I was in a chipper mood.

"In the tank in hydrotherapy."

"Far out. Got a roach clip?"

"Yeah. I was pretty good."

"Good. Here, let me help you with that." He clamped off the end of the catheter with what we had been using as a roach clip.

"Funny thing you'll find," he said, kneeling at my side and undoing the rubber leg bag straps. "A good paraplegic can swim better than most people."

"Bullshit."

"I swear. Strong arms, shoulders, tapered body, not much weight to drag. Compensations, Willie. There was a paraplegic doctor taught anatomy when I was in training, invited our class up to his place in the country over Memorial Day weekend. He had this big place up in the mountains, thirty acres, all wooded, with a cabin and a creek and a pond—he got around on a golf cart. Well, this guy could outswim every single person in the class."

"Married ones too?"

He winced. "He was married himself. Had this kid named Albie. I got to be pretty good friends with

136

the doctor, and we'd drive up to the country every couple of weekends, him and me and his wife and kid. And the whole drive, Albie would sit in the back of the station wagon, playing with his blocks and singing the same song—'Goin Fwimmin.' Fwimmin in da Fweek. Goin Fwimmin in da Fweek."

I joined in the chorus as Lee got behind the chair, and we sang as we rolled down the corridors, in harmony, to the tune of "Bringing in the Sheaves":

"Fwimmin in da Fweek
 Fwimmin in da Fweek
 Fwimmin in da Fwee-eek
 Fwimmin in da Fweek."

Dwownin

All silvery, the steel and chrome pipes and machines of the hydrotherapy room shine dully in the cool half dark. The tile walls echo our song as we roll to the deep tank sunk into the middle of the tile floor. Lee lifts me from the chair and sets me at the edge of the tank. My feet dangle into the sparkling clear water, silvered by the chrome steel of the tank.

"Okay, just grab the parallel bars," says Lee, reaching up from the tank to lift me down into it. The water is warm, bath warm and chest high. The bars are submerged, hip high. I stand easily between them, buoyed by the water.

"Hands and feet even. Distribute your weight evenly. Okay. Left hand forward. Shift your weight to the left and bring your right leg forward." I kind of throw my right hip forward, and the leg floats along after it, but I can't really feel its weight, nor where the

137

foot is, and my left leg buckles slightly. I start to fall, slip beneath the surface, frozen in surprise, neck mouth nose eyes under water. I sink all the way down, and come to rest, bump, on the bottom of the tank, sitting with a slight list to port, bewildered. I have no idea, it occurs to me, of what to do to get my legs under me, to stand up. I open my mouth as if to ask a question, and get a lungful of water.

I feel myself being lifted up, and find myself choking and spluttering on the edge of the tank.

"You got it about half right," says Lee. "Just as well we smoked that joint—I was right, it would've got wet."

Then he started me going again, and again I hadn't gone a step before I went down.

And again.

And again.

"Lee, I can't do it."

"Sure you can," he said, hauling me out of the tank, bundling me in a robe, drying me off tenderly. "You just have a little more work."

"Drowning ain't work."

"No, in the gym. Getting your arms stronger, and those quads."

"Oh fuck." My good mood had dissolved like meth crystal in a steam room.

"You're going to walk, Willie," said Lee in answer to my unasked questions.

"Surrre," I said.

"Really."

"Just leave me alone."

"Oh fuck," Lee said, "are we going to lose a day of therapy because you're depressed?"

I sat sullenly, silently.

"Tell you what. You're about ready for a thera-
peutic visit."

"A what?" I was intrigued.

"You want to come over to my apartment for
lunch? I'll get you a pass, it's just around the next building, we'll get stoned, listen to some music. Okay? Okay.
You get dressed, I'll go square things with the manage-
ment."

And he left me off at my room.

The outside world?

Far out!

(I'm terrified.)

12

Peeking Around

I sat back deep into the couch at Lee's, took a looong toke, and looked out the picture window to the Bronx, spread out seventeen stories below us, and farther off to Manhattan, tall-standing towers shining in the sun to the south.

I was just goddam exhausted, not physically (all I did was set there and get pushed), but emotionally I felt whipped to shit.

I'd spent the whole ride watching myself in the wheelchair—ass high in the elevators—convinced that everybody who was *not* looking at me was avoiding me, and that everyone who *looked* was staring. I'd noticed the way my knees fell together in the chair, the way my slippered feet splayed out. I'd considered and rejected pretending that I was really healthy—just in for a knee operation, y'know. No sir, this boy here is one of yer genuwine cripples—and that was why they all stared/looked away.

It was only a short trip—down the elevator (Ryder was situated on a hill behind the main building, so it's down . . .) to the lobby, through the noontime crowd, across a mall, and up to Lee's—but it felt awful goddam long.

Lee helped me transfer to the couch—my arms trembled like an old man's—introduced me to his old lady, Kathy, tried to make some conversation, but I was shell-shocked, pale and shaken, so he just left me with a joint and retired to the kitchen to help Kathy with lunch.

And I took, like I say, a looooong toke, and another, and a third, and—say! this is good dope!—felt the terror ease out of my bones. By the time mine hosts returned from the kitchen I was actually able to look at them, wasn't turning my head away in shame and pain and confusion.

"You're one resilient son-of-a-bitch," said Lee.

"Hunh?"

"Some people get set back for days after their first time out."

"It's not just me?" Somehow I felt better.

"Shit no, man, that first ride's a pisser."

"We have nothing to feeya . . ." said Kathy, and I looked at her a little more carefully. She had dark hair cut short, in little loops close to her head, the overall effect of her face was alive, sexy, would not attract attention, but could hold it. I felt good for Lee because I wanted the best for him.

We got considerably more stoned then, and talked —the room was set up for talk—and stared idly down at the city. We listened to music. Lee put on the Byrds and in my mind's eye the Chestnut Mare and I floated lazily through the picture window to drift down through the blue sky to the city below.

I was sad when the time came to go back to the

hospital, but I wasn't scared. Somehow the calm of the afternoon, the company of a couple of friends, had returned me to being *me,* instead of a crippled stranger in a wheelchair.

I finished the afternoon in the gym, lifting weights. Dumbbells. Fifteen pounders.

The Jewish Colleen

Let me set you a pretty puzzle.

It has just a few pieces. One is how you put your socks on when you can't reach your feet. Another (fits right next to it) has to do with your shoes. This next piece here is pulling your pants on over your ass while you're still sitting on it.

When you've put all the pieces together, you're dressed.

I never would have been able to complete the puzzle without the good-natured help of Joan Kelly, the OT. Or maybe I would've, but I would have looked awful funny with my socks dangling from my toes and my pants zipped to my knees.

Joan Kelly. The Jewish colleen. Short, round (not too), dark-haired, light-eyed, button nose. A perfect colleen. The name was the result of grandfather Kelistovich's encounter with a playful immigration man.

The problem, I discovered, was that with the brace (and dire consequences were predicted if I ever took it off—I imagined, from the warnings, turning into a hunchback quadraplegic dwarf) I couldn't reach my feet. And my legs were neither limber enough nor the muscles strong enough to lift my feet to my lap. So there I was, in pajamas, or getting my clothes changed lying on the bed, like a toddler. Damned embarrassing.

Then Joan appeared, in answer to a summons from Dr. Hassel, and taught me to dress myself. Also damned embarrassing.

Except she never let me get embarrassed. Instead of letting me act like I was on a ridiculous quest with grim moments, which was my natural inclination, she behaved as though it was an oh so serious important mission with light moments.

The mission, of course, was self-sufficiency for me, but I tended to lose sight of it after, say, the twentieth time I missed my toe with the mouth of a sock.

Joan never lost sight of it. She came equipped with all the gadgetry the great predatory American surgical supply industry could invent and overprice.

Like the EZ Glide Kombination Extendo Grip and Roach Klip, a stick with a coat hook on one end and a huge alligator clip on the other.

Y'know, in three days, I could dress myself top to toe in twenty minutes. There were still some things I couldn't do, though, and Joan backed me up when as a result of one of these, they threatened (emptily) to drum me out of Ryder.

It was this goddam part-time pregnant nurse. On Sunday. Ten A.M. Dr. Woodson was out in the garden with his wife, and I was getting dressed.

All except for my shoes. I realized with a flash of annoyance that the night crew had put them up in the top shelf of the closet upon sweeping up last night.

So I rang for the nurse, and this Patricia answered the ring. I wasn't that fond of her, but pregnancy had softened what I assumed to have been her predatory features, and I had no reason to dislike her.

"Could you get me my shoes?" I asked.

She probably didn't even know why she responded, "Say please."

I know I didn't know at the time why I began screaming. But I did, and even though I was out of practice I managed to call her, without stopping to choose words, a slimy fucking bloated pig's ass of a cunt, and punctuated the phrase with a well-thrown water glass that burst against the door behind her fleeing back.

The next nurse that peeked in got me my shoes, and intimated that the shit was really going to come down.

And come down it did, in the person of the Sunday nursing supervisor, the regular nursing supervisor, a complaint, a report, and an informal hearing in my room.

It wasn't until the hearing that I told my side of the story. I had waited for utmost effect and long-reaching consequences—patient but inevitable was my wrath. As I had suspected, Patricia had left out the part about "Say please," the revelation of which (told with downcast eyes by the wounded innocent) horrified all these amateur psychologists to whom my self-image was a matter of paramount importance.

The nurse, I am happy to say, was let off with a severe reprimand and forced apology.

I accepted graciously.

Dr. Woodson Meets the Shoeman

Next morning a small man with a mustache came down to the gym to meet Dr. Woodson and me.

144

"Looks like a shoe salesman," said the doctor. I checked him out, neat hair, fleck of dandruff, three-piece suit—yup.

Turned out he was, too. Sort of. He was from the orthopedic company, and he was to fit my roomie and me with braces—full leg for him, calf height for me.

He told us, kneeling to measure, that he would have to take our shoes away for a few days to fit them with sheaths into which the braces would lock. He said there were two ways to do it—either drill holes in the heels, or build the brace into the shoe. The latter, of course, was slightly more expensive, but considering the advantages . . .

"What advantages?" Dr. Woodson asked, his deep voice booming.

"Well." The man was slightly startled. "Cosmetic. Cosmetic reasons."

"What the hell you mean, cosmetic?" The doctor forced him.

"So the braces don't show. So if someone saw you sitting at a table, they wouldn't . . ."

"Wouldn't what?" I joined in.

"Well . . ."

"I know." Then Dr. Woodson pitched his voice mockingly high—an old biddy. "Do you think there's anything wrong with Dr. Woodson, Helen. After all, we haven't seen him walk in twenty years."

"No Priscilla," I raised my voice to match his. "How can there be anything wrong? His shoes look perfectly normal."

The shoe salesman completed his measurements and left. Our laughter faded to occasional chuckles throughout the afternoon, and thereafter we used as a catch phrase when one of us was particularly down: "There's nothing wrong with you, Willie. Your shoes look fine."

Message from Don Juan

Dear Capt Rico

Thanx fr yr letter. Okay, I hear you, I can understand your not wanting to visit—I guess everybody has some things they can't do. Sometimes I think it shows weakness on yr part, but sometimes, some really bitter times, it's the easiest thing in the world to understand.

Like today.

The physical therapists here have a term they use for terminal patients. They say, Can't you hear the angel's wings? Or if verbal communication is ruled out, flap their hands at their shoulders.

And you can really feel it. Like today, it's raining out (one wall of the PT gym is glass doors and windows that look out on the patio). They have the lights turned on full, it's indirect lighting, but still, you know that depressing feeling of fluorescent lights on a rainy day?

And three times I see Lee (my PT) flap his hands at Stanley (another) and three times I look over at the doorway, and three times . . .

An old man in a wheelchair with blue lines drawn on his head. The blue lines mean cobalt treatments, for brain tumor. When they start doing cobalt treatments on your brain tumor, it's time to buy your jelly beans one at a time. And with Lee's help, I can see the angel of death floating right over the guy's head.

Then Lee starts him to walking (what else can

they do?)—they have to start him and stop him—
he has a slight list to port, so they send him around
the room counterclockwise, and you can see the
angel circling counterclockwise, slowly, over his
head.

Then they bring in an old old lady in a wheelchair,
whose days, one might assume from her age alone,
would be numbered even if she was healthy, which
she isn't by any stretch of the old imagination. I see
Stanley look at her chart and flash the angel wings at
Lee. So now there's two angels in the room. This
one hovers over her as Stanley tries to teach her to
push her own wheelchair. But she—her head lolls
over to one side, and in her head, as Lee says, there
just ain't nobody home.

I can almost hear her angel laughing.

Then they bring in a little kid of almost inde-
terminate gender—I think a little girl—pale com-
plexion, listless eyes, occasionally she'll get a burst
of manic jangly energy, and flail around in her
chair, but mostly she just sits there. And sure
enough, Daisy the aide looks at her chart and calls
out across the room to Lee, "Another angel."

Thus ended my physical therapy for the day.
I dropped my dumbbells (twenty pounders now)
and fast-assed it back to my room. Lee came by later
and pointed out that if I let things like that throw
me, I'll be here twice as long.

After all, he said, the hospital's where our society
sends people to die. They gotta be *some*place.

Depressing thought.

See ya when I get out.

Love,
Willie

147

Dear Willie,

Don Juan says everybody's death waits over their left shoulder. Him, those old people, me, you. So cheer up.

Love,
Rico

Ballin the Jack

The bars. The parallel bars. Wheel to the end, stare down them, long as railroad tracks, seeming to meet in the distance.

Lock the chair. Flip the chair legs to the side, out of the way. Look up at the bars. Reach up and grab them awkwardly, thumbs inside.

Deep breath.

Push down with the arms. Down! Hard! Hard as you ever pushed anything. And tense the quadriceps.

And up you come. But at the top, what? What balance? You can't feel your feet, you look down at them. Together? Wrong! Try to spread them apart. Push up harder with the arms (now at your side, gripping the bars at hip height) to take weight off a leg to move it to the side. Oh, too far. Oh fuck. At the hips, stiffly, you start to fall to the side.

Bang, your elbow strikes the bar.

Lee steadies you, helps you get centered. Swaying. Odd sensation standing without feet. Like stilts.

Now the hard part. Slide right hand forward. Kick left leg. Not far enough. Whoops. Too far. Oh fuck. Saved again.

Then left hand. Slide. Lift right leg, kick forward.

Awright! Three more steps with each foot, and you're at the end of the bars.

Slide kick. Easy enough. To the end.

Here's Lee with the chair. What the fuck? How do you get back in? All you can do it seems is collapse forward into it.

No, grab the arms. Lower.

Slowly or you're on your ass. Twist your back. Now put your right hand over on the left arm as you twist, then left hand to right chair leg, now right leg over to the left.

Now you're sitting a little sideways. Yeah. You can figure out the rest.

Bring your left foot over, switch your left hand back.

And that's what they call ballin the jack.

It'll get easier.

The Old Folks at Home

My days are taking on a regularity that I find far from displeasing. Awakened for pills at eight o'clock, I find myself coming to consciousness enough to swallow, then sliding back into the arms of ol' Morph so smoothly that I sometimes don't even remember awakening.

Cold breakfast around nine thirty, down to PT by ten, work till noon. The work is tripartite by nature —one third of the time I lift weights, twenty-five-pound dumbbells now, sitting in my chair, mostly pushing-type exercises to prepare my triceps (the muscle that runs down the back of the upper arm) to bear my weight on crutches.

Another part of my time is leg work, which I also find rewarding—my strength grows measurably day by day. Lee has me lie on my back on a mat for the leg work, hooks boards with roller-skate wheels under my heels, hangs sandbags over my ankles. I draw my heels toward me, bending my knees (easy enough) or slide my legs apart (difficult, those muscles are weak) and together. Or I lie on my side and bring my legs backward and forward. The rollerboards are to help overcome friction—without them the muscles are too weak to move the legs at all in some directions—but every day the weight of the sandbags increases and soon I won't need the wheels.

The third division of the work is practice walking —at the parallel bars until I am stronger and my own braces have arrived (these are temporary). This is the most rewarding of all, and I spend all the time Lee allows at the bars, swinging to and fro along them like a possessed monkey, until other patients need the bars.

I eat both lunch and dinner in my room, usually with Dr. Woodson, and am pleasantly surprised to find myself with a heavy appetite each day. I don't order the regular hospital meals—I've had enough of them—but have the kitchen send up sandwiches and coke for lunch (generally) and spaghetti for dinner. This is with the advice and consent of Dr. Hassel, who, no nutritionist, is of the "as long as he's eating" school of pragmatists.

Her point is well taken, too, as I am beginning to put on some weight, broaden at the shoulders and upper arms, am beginning to resemble somewhat less a sophomore at Dachau. Part of my admissionary examination here had been a weigh-in upon a horizontal bed-patient scale, and I had been not a little startled to discover that, even with a fifteen-pound cast, I weighed only a hundred and seventeen. You can do the subtraction yourself, and come out with a very unhappy-looking figure for a five-foot-eight boy who's just turned twenty.

I daresay I'd have dropped below the three figure mark had I been forced to eat in the dining room with those other inmates who could manage it, but I explained my aversion to Dr. Hassel, and she dug my problem.

Which was largely one of lack of empathy with my fellows, and a slight curdling of the milk of human kindness. But I yam what I yam.

I tried the patients' dining room once, the day after the cast was removed, and lost my appetite for forty-eight hours.

Lemme tell you it was heavy.

I wheeled into the room, which was entered right across from the nurses' station, and I daresay I visibly paled at the scene.

It was a nice enough room. Pastel walls, indirect lighting, lunchroom-type round tables and one-piece pastel molded-plastic chairs comprised one half; Saarinen chairs and bookshelves the other. At noon, the tabled section was filled up with ancient cripples—I was the youngest by forty years, and in my youthful isolation I felt quite the interloper.

They were all grouped around the tables, some in the folding chairs, most in wheelchairs, and they were waiting. For lunch? To die?

I don't know, but their heads were turned away, eyes dulled (several were on anti-depressant drugs), they weren't talking to each other, nor even looking. Just . . . waiting; here an old man with one stricken arm in a sling and face drawn in stroke; here an amputee; this woman is obviously not playing with a full deck, not wrapped too tight ahem kaff kaff as they say.

God, judgments, judgments—I can't clear my head and see them as people, one maybe or two, but these great hopeless numbers—twenty of them, sitting slumped in chairs waiting to gum mushy food in order to gain strength . . . for what?

Then, too, my subconscious must have been making some mighty quivery connections—I mean, I could make all the judgments I wanted, here I was still, among them, to the casual observer one of them, younger for sure, but that a difference in detail, not kind.

My spirits were not improved particularly when the food arrived. The procedure was as follows: The kitchen aides wheeled in a cabinet of labeled trays, read the name off the trays, and waited. Waited for the patient to respond to his/her name, but most didn't, and the Ryder staff would identify each tray's recipient, or, if the name was new or unfamiliar, read through the wristlets to match food to human.

They didn't even answer to their names!

Then they began eating, and I could feel my unease descend from the back of my mind to the pit of my stomach.

Some fed themselves, spooning mush to mouth or environs, gumming open-mouthed, food smearing faces, greasing chins, soaking neck-tucked napkins, plopping to floor. The staff performed admirably, but most of their time was taken up in feeding the old folks too far gone to feed themselves—they hadn't the manpower to mop up, too.

Twenty of them—of us, rather—grouped around round tables in a pastel room. I couldn't eat, couldn't watch, couldn't not watch, and then the old woman next to me leaned toward me and spoke to me in a confidentially loony manner.

She was largely bald, with wisps of gray hair, older than the stones in the garden, toothless, her loose wrinkled lips covered with strained peas, and she leaned close to me, and, as I strained to understand, gabbyhayesed to me the following speech:

"I would like for you to call my son for me, four four one three two one four. Call him and tell him to come get me." Here she poked me in the ribs. "He'll give you your nickel back, don't worry about your nickel." Then a Ben Gunn arm pinch. "Call my son, they won't give me a nickel. Please."

I leaned away, she leaned closer, began the rap again, same rap, same number, same poke, same pinch —surprising strength in that withered talon—and my feeling of unreality gave way to nameless terror and swirled around with a sort of identity crisis—Who am I? Am I one of these—swirled and increased in pressure round and round in my head, mixed with loathing, for them and me, and nausea, until sproingsproing-sproing, I threw my chair into reverse and fled the room.

I looked behind me not at all, afraid, perhaps, of turning into a pillar of aged cripple, and as I left, the old woman's monologue blended into the dull clatter of silverware and gurgle-splish of gummed food.

And since then it's been sandwiches and spaghetti in my room with Dr. Woodson, whose humanity was no more all-encompassing than my own.

Kandy-Kolored Etcetera

Merry Fucking Christmas, ho ho ho, and Santa Claus in the person of the shoe salesman—the goodies unwrapped are shining stainless aluminum and fresh vinyl and Naugahyde, and my head fair spins in straps and spokes and cuffs and gadgets and widgets, instruction books and warranties.

I can hardly wait to go out and play in the snow.

The big present is my very own wheelchair. We had ordered it special, Dr. Hassel, Lee, Joan, and I, after a conference, and it was a beauty—an Everest and Jennings Premiere (the Cadillac of wheelchairs) with custom-built extras.

It was built a little lower and a little narrower than the factory model, for greater maneuverability, with deluxe, slightly padded ribbed Naugahyde back and deluxe seat cushion, top of the line brakes and lock system, crutch cup and loop at the back—a tan and steel beauty that rolled smoothly, easily, silently, could turn on a dime, and topped out at . . . well anyway, I was quite pleased with it.

Braces arrive too, this Friday morning, aluminum, with leather where the cuff at the top comes into contact with my calves (with where my calves would have been had they not been largely atrophied away), built into my black Weyenberg Massagic shoes.

And crutches, too—adjustable aluminum bent Canadian Lofstrans, with forearm cuffs and white rubber around the handles.

Now that I am, like any Amurrican soljer, equipped to the teeth, we'll see to what avail all this basic training has been.

When?

As soon as possible.

13

I Love a Parade

So it was that in the second week of October, a visitor to the Ryder Rehabilitation Center of New Canaan Hospital might have been audience to an enthralling spectacle, a three-man parade. Parade marshal is a towering black man—skin dark as an eggplant except for a lighter tan patch around the face (where an oxygen mask and goggles had protected him from the flash fire of his burning fighter plane during a WW II crash), a long lean man with that curiously lighter face set grimly, powering himself along with full-length wooden crutches, muscling along his obviously useless legs—pushing, dragging on strength alone and determination.

Next in line is a young white boy, stepping in contrast almost delicately, moving one bent metal crutch in tandem with the opposite braced leg. His once tight jeans hang loosely from his waist and bag around thin thighs; they are split at the ankle to fit over the braces. He gives off an aura of gaunt intensity and amusement—long dark brown hair falls in his eyes and every few steps he blows it away from his face. His eyes are light green, shining from a prison-pale face, darting from place to place to take in everything, more often than not crinkling in amusement either at his surroundings or from some unfathomable inner entertainment. His movement, not powerful, is perilous— he, more than the black man, is in precarious balance despite the greater strength of his legs, and from time to time must be steadied by the third man in the parade.

This last is short, dark, walrus-mustached, has heavily muscles shoulders and arms, deep chest, and moves with a weight lifter's characteristic flat-footed spring-thighed walk. He pushes easily with one hand two empty wheelchairs locked in file, and with the other hand steadies the boy.

The black man is Dr. Woodson, the bright-eyed boy (ahem!) is me, and that's Lee bringing up the rear.

I love a parade.

And I would like to caution our imaginary visitor not to take too lightly our spectacle. For all that it wants in trappings—bunting and banners, brass bands and balloons—it's taken an impossible, an unconscionable amount of work to get this parade, the first of its kind, under way, and in any event, all the trappings are amply supplied by my imagination: tricolor bunting; Famous Cripple banners; brass bands pealing heavenward the golden notes of Just a Closer Walk with Thee; giant balloons in the likeness of Roy Campanella, anchored with great difficulty earthward by hordes of struggling newly uniformed Macy employees.

Back in our room, Dr. Woodson and I collapsed in our beds with the same exhausted sigh.

"Whew." The doctor spoke first. "We made it."

"Didn't even need the chairs."

"Glad they were there, though."

"Yeah." It had been a comfort to know we wouldn't have had to collapse to the hard hall floors had we flunked the great test. "My legs are killing me."

"My arms feel like I did five hundred pushups."

"I got blisters on my hands."

"Me too."

"But we made it."

"Yup." Finally, proudly. "We made it."

Tail-Eating Tales

That evening, by way of celebration, Dr. Woodson and I decended into the nether depths of stonedness out in the garden. It was as quiet as the city gets, just the gentle whoosh of nighttime traffic in streets shining wet from a brief sunset shower. We sat alone on the concrete patio in our wheelchairs, surrounded by empty wrought-iron garden furniture, angled toward each other around a low toadstool-shaped concrete table.

We'd each scored an ounce of grass that week, he from his cousin (a photographer for Time-Life), me from my friend Ernie, who'd come visiting after hours, fresh from his dealing rounds. Ernie's shticks that week were generosity and lighting—the latter evidenced by the Christmas lights he carried in his case along with the neatly wrapped ounces, and with which he festooned himself in the bathroom where we sampled his wares. "Why the lights?" I asked him. He said he liked lights. Dr. Woodson kept watch for us from his bed.

His generosity he displayed by laying on me the

aforementioned lid, and so it was that Dr. Woodson and I, this night, were able to be uncharacteristically profligate with our dope, each with his own joint, smoking them like cigarettes, gesturing extravagantly as we caught each other up on our life stories.

". . . Just once," the doctor was saying in his deep voice. "For a night. I was driving in my Porsche, drunk as hell, couldn't even see the road, and I got pulled over.

"The cop said, what the hell are you doing driving a car? and I said that even a fool like him could see I was too drunk to walk. So I spent the night in the Detroit jail.

"Oh, and once I was in the stockade in North Africa. We integrated an officers' club, and got served, then locked up. It was only for a night—when Ben Davis found out about it, he raised holy hell. Anyway, our squad was short enough on pilots, for all the niggers they let through OCS."

Well, I didn't have a whole lot of life story to match his, but with the aid of an inspired metaphoric imagination and an inspired joint all to myself, I managed to make a pretty good narrative of the first Jefferson Airplane concert I'd seen, with Jorma stalking center stage with leonine mane and intensity; Jack doing his insane red Indian back-and-forth two-step, eyebrows flapping wildly; Grace and Marty snarling at each other, each shrieking higher in joyful competition. I told him about the excitement, the light shows in the dark, communal public dope-smoking, that were so newly strange and wonderful then, and he caught some of my enthusiasm.

I daresay we felt closer that night, closer for the long march together, for the shared karma, made bro-

thers by crushed spinal cords. Close enough to uncover
the secret fears we had both kept buried far down in
the loneliest black holes in our minds.

"Have you had any hard-ons yet?"

"A couple. Hurts with the catheter in. Can't feel
too much."

"I ain't had *nothin* yet." His usual careful phrase-
ology was by the board.

"Well, there hasn't been much sexy around."

"That's the thought that keeps me going. When
I'm home in bed with my old lady . . ." His eyes glazed
over with sentiment. "You met her yet? Of course you
did . . . she is sooo baaad." He gave a little jive head
fake and eyeball roll and we both laughed. "She's
coming to pick me up Friday."

"Pick you up?"

"I got a weekend pass."

"You lucky bastard."

"Yeah." He laughed sharply. "Which gives me
two more days to bullshit myself that I'm still a man."

"Jesus Fucking Christ," I scolded, from a wisdom
born of nineteen years of life and fervid reading of the
Playboy Adviser. "The surest way of not getting it up
is to worry about it."

"Makes one think of the Ouroboros, the snake that
eats his own tail: You think you might be impotent, so
you worry, so you're impotent, so you think you might
be impotent. And so on."

"That's it!"

"What's it?"

"Eating your own tail." I was positively inspired.
"First thing you do in bed is you go down on her. Give
her absolutely the best head you can, really get into
it. Turn her on, take both your minds off your own

159

worries, voilà! You'll probably wind up with an erection so big you could pole-vault with it."

I refrained from pointing out that he had nothing left to lose.

The Tiger's Asshole

It would've been hard to explain to a visitor why Lee was taking my crutches away, leaving me to (necessarily) fall down on a mat in the middle of the gym.

Well, not all that hard. He was checking off a list of things I had to learn before I could go home for a weekend visit. One of them was learning how to fall. Not so hard. Another was learning how to stand up. Harder.

I hadn't yet the upper arm strength (impetus) or hip and lower back muscles (balance) to get up from the floor. Which didn't mean I flunked the test. Nope. I just had to get in some practice crawling (not so hard), to a wall I could lean on, or a rail I could pull on; then I could get to my feet.

Better yet would be not to fall at all, but that ambition seems somewhat unrealizable.

Another thing I had to learn to do was to climb stairs. We practiced, at first out in the back hallway, and I found railed stairs no problem—no more difficult than walking, if more tiring.

But stairs without rails proved impossible first time around, and to satisfy Dr. Hassel's concern that I be able to escape in a fire, I had to bump up and down a flight on my ass. Easy. Humiliating, but easy. Especially since I'd already lived the scene vicariously during Sunrise at Camp Ralph Bellamy.

"Okay, let's try one more thing before lunch," Lee suggested, and I was game.

We left the gym by way of the small outpatients' waiting room, out the electric eye door, and as we hit the heat, I remembered one more of my blessings I had forgotten to count—the air conditioning. Indian summer.

In the circular drive that served the entrance of Ryder, the heat took my breath, and when we rolled to the staff parking lot, the sun glinting off the parked cars made me squint at first.

"Jesus," I said, "I forgot about what the real world felt like."

"You could use a little sun, son," suggested Lee. "You look like you've been in stir for six months."

"I have." We stopped beside an old Plymouth Fury. "Your car?"

"Joan Kelly's. We practice with it." He unlocked it, opened the passenger door wide, and showed me how to angle my chair to the seat, shift my weight, slide over; then how to stow my chair in the back. The door handles and upholstery were hot to the touch, it took me three heaves to get the chair put away, and after one transfer in and back I was limp with exhaustion and soaked with sweat.

"Good enough," said Lee, "but next time you forget to lock the wheels, I'm not going to remind you. I'm gonna let you fall on your ass."

"What are friends for?" I asked, irrelevantly and suggested we get back inside and soak up some cold.

"Speaking of friends, where's Dr. Woodson?" Lee asked.

"He had a weekend pass."

"He swore on a stack of Bibles he'd be back Sunday night."

"You know Woodson. He'll be back when he's goddam good and ready." Buzz click, the door opened to our bidding, just as, skreee, shriek, a Toronado rounded the driveway on two wheels and jolted to a halt outside the Ryder entrance. I rolled into the lobby, turned around 180 degrees, and (buzz click) rolled on out the door again, in time to greet Dr. Woodson while Lee went around to the Toronado's trunk to unship the doctor's wheelchair. The doctor's wife left the driver's seat to help.

Whew. She did look good enough to eat—beige skin, moved like a cat, legs so long it took forever for her to get them out of the car. She looked even better than last time I'd seen her, three days ago, when she'd come to pick the doctor up—her color was better and some of the tension seemed gone from her eyes.

The doctor, when he noticed me—which was not until he was already seated in his chair, such was the intense concentration with which he handled the transfer—gave me a big grin and a surreptitious thumbs up. Then he gave his wife a big kiss good-bye, and we rolled inside to the blessed cool of the lobby, down the hall to the residential wing, past the scolding of Nurse Taliaferro, to our room, where lunch awaited us.

Then, alone, I tugged his sleeve. "You made it?"

"Willie," he said, and it felt good to hear his voice—I'd missed him, "at first it was like trying to stuff a cooked noodle up a tiger's asshole . . . but we made it. She won't have to seek her pleasures elsewhere."

I wet a finger and struck it steaming on an imaginary blackboard. "Hissss," I said. "Score one for our side."

Next morning, Tuesday it was, I woke with a bug in my britches. Figuratively of course. A fixed idea that accompanied me through breakfast and was pretty well implanted by the time I got down to PT.

Lee nodded hi to me, absorbed in instructing a stroke victim in the use of her useless left arm, and cocked his head over to the weight racks. I shook my head, and he raised his eyebrows. I shook my head again, and he held up one finger. "Be with you in a minute," he said, and was no more than five.

"What's up?" he asked. "Tired of the weights?"

"I decided I want to walk out to the car when I go home Friday."

"I don't know," he said. "You haven't walked outside yet. It's harder than you think."

"We got four days to learn."

"We do, do we?"

"I decided."

He laughed. "Okay."

Take one. We rolled out to the lobby, I locked my chair, unsheathed my crutches from the cup in the back of the chair, swung the chair legs out of the way, and stood, swaying slightly. I adjusted the forearm grips of the crutches.

"So far, so good," said Lee. Then I walked, step by step, in the four-point gait, crutch and opposite leg, out the electric door. The heat was as bad as the day before, but not as much of a shock.

"Okay," said Lee, inconspicuous, but no more than a step away. "Let's say the car is right at the curb."

I nodded and stepped out boldly with my right foot,

then moved up the right crutch and made to drag the left foot forward. But the linoleum and carpeting inside had not prepared me for the friction of the concrete, and the tip of my left shoe caught and dragged, and I began to pitch forward. In the wink of a bird's eye, Lee caught me by my Southern Comfort belt, and I dangled from the waist, held up only by his strength. Holding me in one hand, he brought the chair up with the other, then let me fall backward into it.

"Surprise," he said.

"Fuck off," I said. "Let's try again."

"This afternoon," he promised, "if you do some more weight work this morning."

"Sheeit."

"The stronger you get, the better you'll be able to hold yourself up if you trip like that."

Grudgingly I let him wheel me back into the cool, comparatively dark lobby, and went back to work in the gym.

We tried another take after lunch, and I made it halfway to the curb.

By Wednesday morning I was able to walk to the curb. By Wednesday afternoon I could make it to the curb, get into a car (lent unsuspectingly by an obliging visitor with the poor judgment to leave his car unlocked), get out of the car, and walk back to the lobby.

By Thursday afternoon I could walk from gym to car.

By Friday morning I was ready to screw bears and wrastle Indian maidens.

Friday afternoon Dr. Hassel had the pharmacy send me up a weekend's worth of pills, had me fitted out with a fresh catheter, leg bag, and night urine bag, signed half a dozen pink and green forms, and I was ready to go home.

My mother was so surprised and happy when I walked to the car to meet her (with Lee close behind, carrying my suitcase, ready to grab me) that she broke down and cried.

Which was, after all, what I'd planned the whole surprise for.

I felt awful good.

14

Goin' Home

The Indian summer heat of the week had given way to a pleasant premonitory autumn chill, sweetened nonetheless by a warm sun, and everything stood out just a little bit sharper than I could remember—the colors a little brighter, like a Technicolor movie, the air a little crisper.

OOOeee, but autumn was a nice time to come home. My mother zipped the red Buick Skylark along at a fair pace, glancing over from time to time to see whether the ride was making me nervous.

Nervous? Who had time to be nervous? Here was the world, gone so long, come back to me now.

"Far out. They still doing construction of the Expressway?"

"Always."

I lit a cigarette, took a long pull, opened my window to the traffic sounds, trying somehow to take it all in.

Six months, and it was all still there, the Expressway, our exit, the small shops in the village, and the great supermarket city.

Then, on our street, I found myself swallowing hard at the way the sunlight and bright golden and red leafed trees cast mottled shadows on the street.

"The roses?" I asked my mother.

"Still going strong." We turned into the bluestone gravel driveway, and my mother executed a three-point turn and backed down the driveway to bring my door flush with the short cement walk.

"Where's Judy?" I asked, and as if in answer, I heard a little voice calling my name, and saw my kid sister come running down the path that connected us with the neighbors.

God in heaven, the six months that had left the world unchanged had altered my sister almost beyond recognition. I remembered her as a baby, but now she was tall as a fire hydrant and her once long black hair was cut in a pageboy that accentuated the roundness of her face, made her look like a china doll.

"Willie Willie Willie Willie Willie." I opened the car door and she jumped into my arms. We snuggled and kissed for a minute, then I said, okay, lemme get inside, and she backed off into the flower bed lining one side of the walk, and I twisted around and grabbed my crutches from the back.

I stood, using the car for support, and then shifted my weight to the crutches, headed for the door, a dozen steps away. No Lee spotting. One at a time, Willie, take em one at a time.

After three or four steps I glanced over at Judy (my mother was bringing the chair up behind me) and saw her staring at me, huge brown eyes open round, mouth pursed, with me every step of the way.

I made it up to the two red brick steps and realized

they had no rail. Oh fuck. Well, damned if I'm gonna bump up on my ass for two steps. I lifted the left crutch, pitched forward, caught the doorjamb with my left hand, crutch hanging from my forearm. I pulled and pushed myself up, with left hand and right crutch, and stood swaying in the doorway for a minute. By then the wheelchair was ready and I sank down into it. Then Judy jumped up into my lap, not shy of the chair at all.

"Okay," I said, "hold on, let's take a ride," and I wheeled through the house, room by room, taking in everything.

Finally I wheeled into the den, where there was an enormous, brand-new color TV. "Welcome home," my mother said, her dark glasses in place to hide the tears. Judy was crying and hugging me too, and damned if I didn't start bawling myself.

Welcome home.

There's not too much more to tell about that first evening home. I did nothing that everybody doesn't do on a quiet Friday night, but everything was so familiar, and strange, and wonderful, that I wheeled around the house in an unbelieving daze.

I sat in the deep soft armchair that we still called Dad's chair, though he was two years dead.

We ate off TV tables in the den, and as the night grew chillier, my mother built a small fire in the fireplace.

We watched the bright vivid colors on the TV, pictures so bright they made us slightly dizzy, and I climbed down on the floor to roll around with little Judy, and wrestle, and tickle.

Even sitting on the toilet I grew up with was a thrill. I closed the bathroom door, hauled myself with one hand on the windowsill to open the window, and smoked a whole joint. Not that I had to hide—just for old time's sake.

I even took a shit, in my fashion, pulling turds out manually from the paralyzed bowel with a crooked forefinger. Had a brief bad moment then, a buzzing sense of unreality, and a stone-fogged voice in my head said—if this is really you, and you're really home, then what's this? And this? And this? These? Indicating empty wheelchair parked next to the toilet, leg bag sloshing with old urine, thin, braced legs.

But there was still a sensible voice in me, under the smoke, behind the buzzing in my ears, unimpressed by the fact that the shiny green tiles seemed to be advancing and receding under the deadly fluorescent light; and that friendly voice explained calmly, it's still you, no matter what happens to your body. You just feel strange bringing your new body to a home that remembers the old one. But it's still you.

Seemed there was going to be more to this rehabilitation than just lifting weights.

And when I'd left the bathroom, after what seemed like years, Judy was waiting outside the door, begging for another ride in the chair. I pulled a wheely and off we went.

I put her to bed, sang her to sleep with my world-famous Good Night Irene/Go Tell Aunt Rhody medley; said goodnight to my mother; put myself to bed, performing all the catheter irrigation, urine-bag changing, pill-taking rituals I'd come to depend on the nurses for; and slept like a baby, to wake up to the autumn sunshine coming in through the front windows in my room, just like when I was a kid, those oh so long six months ago.

Meet Cripple Willie

The morning, beginning of my first full day out in the world, introduced me to this character I came to call Cripple Willie, who took over my thoughts at what seemed to be random moments, and who, in those bad moments when he was in charge, reduced the rest of me to paralysis.

Like: I get up to the sunshine, perform my many ablutions and adjustments, wheel into the living room, see the sun shining in the big picture windows, making window frame patterns on the carpet. I think—far out, I'll go outside. But as I glance around to see who or what I'll need to go outside—chair? crutches? help?—Cripple Willie cuts in—too hard, you'll fall, don't bother anybody to help you, they'll start to resent you.

Or, my mother's really chirping around the kitchen whistling, cracking eggs with élan, in her element with a bright new orange apron, happy as a pig in shit, and I think, I'll bet she's extra happy because I'm home. Then Cripple Willie points out maybe she's happy in spite of me, and suddenly the wheelchair seems a monstrous encumbrance, and unappetizing unhealthy deformity, and Cripple Willie also suggests that if she turns and sees me wheeling toward her, the smile will drop off her face and crash to the floor in a million pieces.

Or I start to call Capt Rico, thinking my old friend will be glad to see me, but Cripple Willie freezes my finger on the dial, makes me put myself in Rico's shoes and know what a drag it'll be to see me, and I hang up.

I began to see that if I let Cripple Willie call the shots, I'd never get outside, kiss my mother, or call my friends.

I decided to operate under the hypothesis that he was a liar.

So I made the call to Rico, who sounded happy to see me, said he'd show up at six with new super dope, a friend's car, and an extra ticket to the Ravi Shankar concert out at the State College, where before the accident we had both been students.

Another home to revisit.

Of course, at that point, Cripple Willie took over and began warning me of all the difficulties and embarrassments *we*'d have to face if we went out there, but although I couldn't shut him up, he had little power over me once I'd recognized him.

I knew he was a goddam liar.

Rockin Raga

Here we go again. Another careening ride through the Long Island dark, tires screaming, whoops of joy from the six of us at every near miss. Joints fired up two, three at a time—"One for the back seat . . . One for the front seat . . . One for the driver . . . One for the pot . . . Pun! . . . Chuckle . . . Choke."

It was, as the vernacular would have it, dynamite shit.

"Michoacán," Rico explained, crammed in next to me in the front seat of Robby's old Ford. Next to Rico, Robby was driving with his usual dreamy nonchalance, unmindful of traffic and road conditions, but with a lead foot flooring the accelerator.

Trial by fire for me—either I was going to burn through my fear of automobility, or I was going to dissolve into a shivering blob of terror, whimpering like a kicked puppy on the floor.

"Pass the dope, old buddy," was my decision. "Michigan, ey?"

"No, Michoa— for chrissakes Robby!" We jerked back in line. "That was a cop you cut off."

"Sorry."

"S'all right."

"Michoacán," Rico continued, with a sidelong eye-roll at Robby's driving. "It's a province in Mexico."

"You dealing it?" Robby was absentmindedly playing with the bright switch, sending feeble beams jerking off at askew angles into the night.

"Naw, but I can get you some."

"Just an ounce."

"See what I can do."

Rico's brother John and his two friends in the back seat, all semipro football players, had smoked themselves into semiquiet oblivion and sat shoulder to shoulder enjoying the ride. As we headed for the State College, Rico filled me in on some of the gossip I'd missed: student strikes, faculty strikes, construction, busts, the smack invasion—all the depressing crap we'd come to associate with college.

And between the chatter and the dope, sitting in the car with five other seated, sedentary friends, I forgot all about my problem, about the wheelchair in the trunk, about the nagging ache in my back and legs from the unaccustomed exertion of the last two days. Forgot about it, that is, until we pulled in past the security gatehouse at the entrance to the road, and the cop waved us to a parking lot that lay in the opposite direction from the gymnasium where the concert was to take place.

Like a sleepy fool, Robby started heading where the cop pointed, but Rico stopped him with a hand on the wheel. "My friend here is in a wheelchair," he explained to the cop, who came around and looked at me as if expecting some proof—maybe he thought I was in the wheelchair in the car. I rolled up my jeans and showed him the braces, my face flushing red.

"Okay," the cop said, slightly embarrassed himself, "go on ahead," and we drove through the strolling crowd toward the gym, past two more checkpoints, and parked as close as we could to the entrance, which was jammed with milling concert goers.

"Whaddaya think, Willie? Can ya walk it?" I looked at the four marble steps, the twenty-yard uneven flagstone patio in front of the gym entrance, the crowded doorway, and extrapolated from memory the spacious lobby in the gym and the expanse of the gym itself.

"No way."

"No problem." He and Robby unshipped the wheelchair from the trunk, set it up beside the car, and I transferred with a singleness of purpose that blotted from my mind the curious stares of the passersby. Then Rico and John grabbed the chair, lifted it up the steps, and pushed me across the bumpy patio, toward the crowd at the gym doors. John's friends walked a little ahead, clearing the way with a word here, a shoulder there. I felt weightless, insubstantial.

It was the longest ride I had ever taken in my whole short life. There was no useful task I could turn my attention to; I just had to (for christ sake) sit there, pushed through the crowd like a cartful of groceries. The dope was beginning to turn on me in my paranoia, my head buzzed, and the gym itself, as we pushed through the people idling in the lobby, became a universe of pale floating faces looking down at me, then turning away, but I could see, with the eyes that had grown in the back of my head, the eyes of a hunted animal, all the people out of my line of sight staring at me, and I could hear them whispering.

He's just paranoid, you say! It doesn't matter. It felt real to me, so real I felt sick, almost puked, turned pale down to my fingernails, and my hands trembled.

We finally reached our seats on the gymnasium floor. John removed a folding chair next to the aisle, lifting it out of the way like a matchstick, and I rolled in. The lights dimmed as we settled ourselves, and Rico handed me a joint. I toked greedily.

"Thanks," I said. "I needed that."

I took a deep breath and closed my eyes, as in the darkness behind my eyeballs the first sitar notes rippled and flashed electric blue and blinding white laser-dot patterns.

And in my private darkness I relaxed, applauded, laughed, as Ravi Shankar said, like he always does, "If you so enjoyed the tuning up, I am sure you will like the concert even more."

Mood Elevator? No Thanks, I'll Take the Stairs.

I slept the sleep of the righteous that night and well into the next morning, to awaken to the smell of coffee perking and (this here's a subtle one) bagels toasting. Yeah. A kaleidoscope of images, white deli paper oily with orange lox, white bakery bags filled with onion rolls, slabs of cream cheese, whitefish thick and soft as cheese, coffee with heavy cream—the kind of breakfast my father had insisted on every Sunday of his adult life, the kind of breakfast we hadn't had since he died.

It was all there just as I had imagined it, and the Sunday *Times* too. As we ate, though, and as we traded sections of the paper, refilled our coffee cups, and watched TV, in other words, as morning progressed lazily toward afternoon, my mind was visited with a certain disquiet that threw off, ever so slightly, each luscious bite and slow Sunday moment.

I'd had the feeling before, but it took me awhile to place it. Of course! It was like all those Sundays as a kid when I knew I hadn't done the weekend's home-work and that sure as shit Monday was gonna dawn.

I had to be back at Ryder by eight o'clock that night, which meant I had to leave my home by seven. I couldn't even pretend to get sick, like I used to do on the homeworkless Mondays of yore.

I ate most of my favorite dinner (flank steak, mashed potatoes, apple sauce, and Coke from a six-and-a-half-ounce green bottle) without tasting it, dried Judy's tears, ignored my mother's cheerful chatter, and rode back to the Bronx silent and sullen in the passenger's seat.

It all seemed, suddenly, so goddam *unfair*, that I should have to go back—that I should have been there in the first place—and I got an attack of the why-me's that caused me to snap at my mother, ignore the nurses, crawl angrily back into my bed, and wait for Dr. Woodson to return from *his* weekend because I knew I could talk to him.

I fell asleep waiting, and he dragged his ass in at eight in the morning, disgustingly chipper, waking me to a silent sulk that turned me against everyone I came in contact with. Yeah (by way of illustration), I know that last sentence ends in a preposition. Fuck you, what's it to you anyway. Just leave me alone. Leave me alone.

The worst part of this black dog fit I was in was the way it made me treat my friends.

The cycle of relations was a vicious one. My depression was nothing if not dramatic, and it stamped me with delicious agony that would have been obvious to a blind man. So everyone who welcomed me back to Ryder saw something was wrong, and inquired about it.

But what the hell could I say? It's not fair? Why me? Jesus, I saw Marlon Brando in *that* movie. So I turned away, said nothing, and the unrelieved pressure made my throat ache and brought tears to my eyes, and I would have to turn away even farther, to look out a window or at the TV, till I had control.

Nobody got mad at me though—it was all too familiar a scene to the staff here. Which didn't help my disposition any, to have my great pain written off as a stage all cripples go through, a delayed depression. I angrily refused the mood elevators they offered (Librium), bitching that they weren't gonna take away my right to be depressed.

I must've been a real pain in the ass.

I actually managed to avoid significant conversation with any human being for three days.

176

"How ya feeling?"

"Okay."

Or, "D'ja see the seventh game in th' Series?"

"Nope." So everybody left me pretty much alone, while I distilled the pain into an I.D. Fixay: I want out!

Dr. Hassel came by to see me Thursday, clicked in awkwardly on those brown high heels she always wore, lab coat rumpled, lipstick slightly smeared. Her appearance didn't inspire much confidence, nor her slightly distracted manner, but she was a nice lady, and I assumed, from her standing as heir apparent to Dr. Aarons (the seldom seen boss of Ryder) she was a good doctor.

She looked surprised when I asked to speak to her, expecting, I suppose, the same rebuff she had received twice that week. She sat down at the side of the bed.

"What can I do for you, stranger?"

"I wanna get out."

"I should hope so."

"When?"

"I don't know. When you're ready."

"I have to know when or I'm fucking gonna go crazy."

She looked down at her clipboard as if it had the answer to my question, then sighed and spread her hands. She spoke matter-of-factly, laid her cards on the table:

"We can't let you out of here with a catheter. Too dangerous, you'll be infected all the time, kidney damage, can't do it. So we'll get Doctor Steinman in, the urologist, and start to work on that.

"In the meantime, you keep working in the gym, arm work and walking. With the muscles you've got, I think a hundred yards is the minimum you should be able to do before we let you out, otherwise we'd be cheating you."

"So," I reiterated, "when the catheter's out and I can walk a hundred yards, I can go home?"

"With my blessing."

I did a mock benediction and smiled at her all the way out. Disgustingly cheerful, I was.

I mean, practically it didn't mean much. I'd always known I'd get out someday. But shit, a target now, as all the pleasures of outside took their place in real objective time.

A minute later, Joan Kelly stuck her head in the door, asked if I was up for a game of cribbage. Last time she'd asked, I'd told her to go weave a basket, which is a very cruel thing to say to an Occupational Therapist.

So I was glad to make it up to her by letting her beat me. (Ahem.) And before she left, she promised to get hold of a hand-controlled car for me to practice drive with.

"You do have a license?" she asked.

"Naturally."

15

Steinman's Guinea Pig

No sense running through that next month in
detail—it rolled and flowed the way time does when it
has a purpose. During the days I threw my energies into
work—lifting weights, on my back or on my ass, and
walking, walking, walking, until the triceps muscles
screamed.

Evenings and weekends (I didn't feel I was ready
for the disappointment of going home and having to
return again) I buried myself in reading and TV—
classics, mysteries, *Playboy* (skipping the gatefold, for
fear of another painful erection), and any crap the TV
cared to offer.

I was learning to take each day on its own terms,
and it wasn't a bad time at all, except for a certain
anxiety about the damn catheter, and the future of my
private parts.

Dr. Steinman was a pleasant, rumpled man with
white hair that sproinged out around his ears, half
glasses that slipped down on his nose, and a devastat-
ingly bad collection of rote urogenital-related puns
and jokes. "I'm Steinman, I cover the waterfront," was

how he introduced himself, and from somewhere in the recesses of my not inconsiderable intelligence I gathered it was a line he'd used before.

He'd given me no prognosis—let's handle it one step at a time was his philosophy, and I came around to subscribing to it, especially when I learned that each step might well involve some torture or other that I'd just as soon not know about in advance.

One particular horror I remember vividly took place along about the second week of my involvement with Steinman.

In a clean hospital gown, I was wheeled into a small, terribly cold room and placed on a sort of gynecological table, legs spread up and out in stirrups, balls swaying in the breeze. I was surrounded by lethal-looking steel instruments and cold steel machines with glass dials all arrowed and red-danger-lined. I was surrounded also by Steinman, a nurse, an aide, a couple of urological interns, a couple of med students all looking unpromisingly efficient and professional. I've often found obvious professional detachment on the part of medical personnel means it's my pain they're planning to be detached from.

In this case, my instincts were right on. It was a bladder function test. They were going to see how much fluid my bladder could hold, and measure the bladder function at various volumes.

"Let me know when you first feel discomfort," said Steinman; then he turned his attention to the dials and meters and clipboards, and a machine began pumping water into my bladder.

A minute went by. I began feeling full, fuller, real full, and finally waved an arm at the doctor. "Okay," I said, making an effort to keep my voice steady, "It feels uncomfortable," thinking he would stop it then, but no, he just mumbled, "good," jotted down a notation, and kept pumping.

"Hey," I repeated, "it's starting to hurt." My voice was shaky. He nodded, his attention on his charts. "No shit, it hurts man, enough." He ignored me, and I looked down and could see my lower belly getting round and hard. Jesus, I thought, I'm gonna explode, but I tried to stay in control of myself, tried to say calmly, "Stop," but the word came out in a squeak, and I realized that if I so much as opened my mouth again, I was going to start crying.

Naturally, I didn't want to cry in front of all these strangers. Naturally, I started blubbering like a baby, pounding my fists on the table and moaning, unintelligibly no doubt, things like Stop, and Cut it out, and Jesus Fucking Christ.

Everyone was totally oblivious to my pleading. They went on until they reached the predetermined end of the test, by which time I had been reduced to a soggy whimpering blob, then reversed the machine and drained the bladder.

"Looks promising," said Steinman to pale white Willie, and had the nurse give me a shot of Demerol and wheel me back to my room.

It was at that point I stopped asking Steinman what came next on the agenda.

And the Leaves Came Tumbling Down

It was late November now, and the gray skies and bare trees visible through the glass doors that separated

181

the gym from the patio were no longer tantalizing reminders of an unavailable world, but rather threatening reminders of the unpredictability of the nonclimate-controlled, nonramped, directly lit outside.

My shoulders and arms were wonderfully strong now from my work—along the backs of my upper arms the triceps stretched like taut cables beneath the skin, and my shoulders seemed permanently tensed from the layers of muscles. I could easily power myself a hundred yards, and now, instead of the slow four-point gait, I swung my legs through in an even swing, motive power all from the arms, and could move at a reasonable speed and cover a useful distance.

The main hangup now, delaying my release, was the bladder problem, and I was hopeful of persuading them to treat that as an outpatient matter, so that I could avoid being left behind (and alone, as I envisioned it) by Dr. Woodson, whose target date for release was Christmas or thereabouts.

I'd begun experiencing some pain in my bladder, nothing much, a twinge here and there. I assumed it had something to do with the catheter, and refrained from mentioning it for fear it would delay my release. Refrained from mentioning it, that is, until this chilly gray November morning.

I was taking a lap around the gym, weaving around the scattered old stroke victims and diabetic amputees, concentrating on speed and smoothness, economy of motion, when I got hit by a pain that knocked me on my ass.

Literally. I was in midstride, came a pain in the groin that I instantaneously visualized as a razor blade floating in my bladder, slicing at random. I forgot everything I'd learned about balance, the strength drained from my arms, the blood drained from my brain, and I found myself lying on my back, over at the entrance to the hydrotherapy room.

Lee was over by the mats. He saw me fall and grinned at me. After all, one of the first things I'd learned in PT was not to be afraid of falling. But a second glance told Lee that something was wrong, and he hurried over to kneel at my head.

I couldn't breathe, much less talk, so I tapped my bladder, where the pain was, and tried to roll up into a ball.

Lemme tell you, things really started popping in that gym, and I got more attention than a bitch in heat at Westminster. The PT's gathered round, the nurses, Dr. Hassel, and then, eventually, Steinman. They poked and tapped and prodded, and the whole scene passed by me like a slide show—I'd open my eyes, take in the scene, then close them and give myself up to the blackness and the pain.

At length, when they'd satisfied themselves, somebody mercifully gave me an injection, a big one, and I let my old friend, the golden glow, warm me and accompany me into unconsciousness.

I awoke again to the coldness and dimmed lights of X-ray, moaned, and was given more dope immediately, all in one quick flash—wake, X-ray, moan, needle, sleep—and was surprised to find myself when next I opened my eyes in the comfort of my own room, in the hushed dark of a hospital evening.

I was also surprised to find my pubic hair shaved off, but I'd been around hospitals long enough to know what *that* meant.

183

"Good morning, glory," said a familiar deep voice near my head, and I looked over to see Dr. Woodson sitting at my bedside in his wheelchair, a magazine in his lap. "Welcome to the land of the living."

"Doc," I said weakly (he hated to be called Doc, but let it pass), "what the fuck happened?"

"Bladder stones."

"Another operation?"

"Tomorrow."

Here we go again.

Divining the Future

I'm no fucking babe in the fucking woods, man. I been around hospitals long enough. I know what's going to happen tomorrow.

They'll take away my water jug soon after midnight signals the new day.

Then they'll wake me up around six and wash me. And I'll lie there for an hour or so (no breakfast) and I'll think.

I'll picture each of my friends being told I'm dead, which is as far as I'll go with death thoughts.

But from there I'll think ahead to the operation, and see the same frozen Zen picture of the second, the actual moment, that the shining scalpel breaks the flesh.

Try it. Imagine they're going to operate on your arm. Look at the arm. Think of the doctor's hand firmly bringing down the razor-edged scalpel, the blade touches the flesh, there, right there on your arm. Slice. Freeze the frame.

Run it ahead again. A straight black slit in your very arm. Freeze the frame.

Run it. A cut is a cut. Blood wells into the slice. They sponge it up and . . .

Well, you see what I mean. I'll hype myself into fibrillation and lie there like a pop-eyed geek until the nurse comes to bring me my twilight shot.

Which will cool me out all the way down to the role of interested bystander.

A man in green will come with a gurney, and we'll ride through sign-bedecked double doors into a stainless steel land where masked people wear green clothes, and they will give me a green hat.

In the preop room, they will put a tube in my arm while they talk among themselves of other things.

Then they will take me to the OR. The doctor will not be there as yet, most likely. They'll put me on the table and I'll wait in the chilled room until the surgeon enters. He'll say hello and make a joke, I bet, and the anesthetists will say hello and inject the pentothal into the IV tube.

I will feel a bitter taste deep in my throat, and before I can count three I will fall down a deep black hole in space, at the end of which is a circle of light that will shrink to a dot, a point; all black.

Together Again:
God, Lowell, Ali, Patterson, Willie

Willie loves you.

And because I do, I'm going to spare you the agonies of another postop morning. I mean, really, we went through that all before, just review your notes.

But of course, the question still remains, what am I going to tell you about? The fucking hospital room? (I was in a regulation room, way upstairs from Ryder, for the postop week.) Okay. Green walls, chrome rails, TV on the ceiling, and the bathroom smelled, no doubt, of Safeguard deodorant soap. Quelle drag!

Picking up some negative vibes from me, are you? Not surprising. I feel like somebody's playing games with me. I feel like . . . Floyd Patterson—in the first Ali fight.

The role of Mohammed Ali is to be filled, ladies and gentlemen, by God.

Remember how Ali whipped the Rabbit like he was his daddy, but would never quite let the man go down? He would pound Floyd's head into chocolate pudding, then ease off until his man was steady, then start all over again. Sometimes, if he had to, he would go into a clinch and half hold Floyd up until the danger was past. He carried that man twelve rounds just so he could beat him up for thirty-six minutes.

The sports world absolutely marveled at old Floyd; courage, they called it, guts, class, with an occasional "masochist" thrown in from the cheap seats of the new journalism. But I'll tell you, my relationship with God lately has given me just this *tremendous* insight into what it must have meant to have been Floyd Patterson on that night several years ago.

You get landed on real heavy the first time, you figure you're shit out of luck, because that man that's in the ring with you is from the *other corner*, and that's all there is, there ain't no more.

But you feel yourself recovering. "I'm getting stronger, I feel better, it ain't so tough, maybe I can handle this guy after all." Only, of course, it isn't you at all, it's that other fella letting up on you so he can have you for the whole twelve rounds.

Then he comes down on you like a thousand-pound shithammer, and there's not any other guy there, there's just "getting hit," and fuck it, you decide to let your knees fold like they want to, and then there's this other fella holding you up, and "Thank you," you want to say, "Oh God thank you," and you feel very close.

And then that other guy backs off a step, looks you in the eye, and then hits you two jabs in the face and a right under the heart, and there you are again.

There I am again.

Flat on my back, in bed, stitched up the middle like a stuffed roasting chicken.

Oh yeah, Floyd Patterson always claimed he only lost because he had a muscle spasm in his back. Stupid niggers never learn.

And as if all that weren't enough to give me the black ass, there was my roommate, Lowell. The old grad.

Lowell was (to fall back on my bad habit of describing people by detailing their infirmities) the victim, these past twenty years—since he was my age, oddly enough—of one of those progressive bone diseases that necessitated periodic amputations; that had, in fact, cost him both his legs to the thigh. *His* god, I think, was an absentminded old fart just a-sittin on the front porch whittling away on a stick that would grow, as whittling sticks do, shorter and shorter, until it was whittled completely away.

Which was no big deal for God—there was a whole pile of soft kindling beside his rocker on the cosmic porch—but was a drag for the stick. Lowell, of course, was the stick, an old stick, halfway gone, and he liked to pass on some of his whittling-stick wisdom to a fresh green twig of a cripple like me.

Dedicated to Susan

"Willie," Lowell said one particular morning, the second after my operation, the fourth after his, "sometimes I think cripples should only marry cripples."

"Oh?" I said.

"Yup," he nodded, reaching for a Kool on his bedside table. "Take my first wife, Susan. I married her when I was twenty-five. I screwed her every night, and we had three kids. And every morning, seven days a week, I'd get up at six A.M. and go down to that newsstand. I'd sit behind that stand from six thirty in the morning until seven thirty at night, and I'd smile at everybody, and be nice to everybody, and get bedsores on my ass, and have my papers hooked by kids who could run away, and seven times—seven times!—I was robbed at the point of a gun.

"And I had to be a different person. I had to be the cripple-who-runs-the-newsstand, cause that's how everybody looks at you; and how everybody looks at you is who you are.

"But I did it. I don't know, I felt I had to—had to support my wife and kids, had to be a man, that way.

"And after ten years of marriage, she left me. Just said, 'Lowell, I'm leaving.' She had another man.

"I told her, 'Honey, I took good care of you. You never wanted for anything, I was a good provider, we screwed every night, what is it?"

"And she said, '*You* did for *me*? *I* did for *you*! I hauled you around, and bandaged you, and massaged

188

your stumps, and carried things for you because it was always easier for me to do things for you than it was to watch you try to do them yourself. I'm sick and tired of it, the sight of your stumps always did make me sick, and I faked coming anyway, when we screwed. I'm sick and tired of it, and now I got a man who can do everything for himself, and both of us, and the kids, and I'll never have to look at another stump. I'm leaving.'

"You know, Willie, it never once, in those ten years, occurred to me that she felt that way, or that she was taking care of me. I thought I was taking care of my family.

"Well now, my second wife, my present wife, she's got cerebral palsy, we take care of each other. We screw every night, and I pick up the welfare twice a month. And if something's too hard to do, why, we let it be.

"Cripples should marry cripples, Willie. Because the other people? They'll always resent you. No matter what they say."

16

Journey to the Center of the Mind

Winter.

I know New York winters. Sky's the color of Rust-oleum primer gray, and I feel the chill deep inside. Sure, my room, my old room, the room I'd shared with Dr. Woodson is warm, clean starched sheets sandwich me and a thermal blanket tucks me in comfy.

But inside, I'm cold, dead—I just can't fight anymore.

I'd spent two weeks upstairs recovering from the most immediate effects of the bladder operation. I'd watched bloody urine crawl through the clear tubing from the catheter to the plastic reservoir hung from the side of the bed. I'd watched it flowing slowly, dark red mixed with black lumps of clotted blood and yellow protoplasmic pus, and sometimes, idly, I'd toy with the flow—stopping it with a pinch or speeding it along by holding my breath and bearing down.

I'd watched the bandages at my groin stain with blood, then pus—changed each day, stained each day, white to red, red to yellow and red and green. It seemed natural that the products of my body were so disgustingly putrescent. That's what my body's for, I'd thought, that's the bloody fucking progress I've been making, oozing the rotten products of my rotting body. That's what we're all about, me and Lowell with his depressing stories—pus and blood and lying helpless in bed.

Steinman had stopped by each day. He'd tell me each day that I had to drink liquid, had to wash out the bladder, keep it clean, stave off infection, recover quickly. But each day I'd looked away, mumbled, and so he'd kept the IV flowing sugar water into my veins to supply my body with fluid. My veins, though, had by the second week collapsed like my spirit, and he replaced the IV's with the recommendation that I drink a glass of water hourly. At that, I'd made the nurses cajole me, bribe me, threaten me, before I'd sipped down the water—and I'd given them nothing of myself in return, not jokes, not insults, not attention.

I'd gagged each morning on my pills, and the nurses had been kind about mashing them in apple sauce, and spoon-feeding me.

But in spite of myself I'd recovered, at least enough for them to bring me back down here to my room in the Ryder Rehab Center of the hospital. I think Nurse Taliaferro was shocked by my appearance this morning when they rolled me down, still supine, on a gurney.

I've lost weight, I know—I can tell by the way my hipbones stick up so sharply. But more than that, I suspect, my eyes have given me away, for if they reflect what I'm feeling, then they don't sparkle now (when I'm happy, I'm told, they sparkle so) and are ringed with black, are hollow, dark and dull.

The worst part, though, has been this last hour. Before I was just empty. Now I'm deprived. For I've returned just in time to watch Dr. Woodson and his wife pack up his stuff, to watch them laughing and joking, to say good-bye to them.

My buddy, with whom I'd lifted weights, smoked dope, jived nurses, who'd sat by my bed two weeks ago waiting for me to come around after my collapse—my buddy was leaving me alone.

I'm taking it as a personal betrayal. I know it's crazy, but he's letting me down, and it doesn't mean shit to him, he's so bubbly, he doesn't even know how down I am.

He rolls over to my bed, shakes my hand, wrings it firmly with both hands, looks in my face, but I look away, keep my face turned until he's gone, until the door is shut behind him.

Then, alone, I cry, but each sob hurts the incision too much, so finally I lie without moving, without making a sound, and the tears dry on my cheeks.

De Blooze

What they don't understand, what Lee doesn't understand, nor Dr. Hassel, nor Joan, is just this: it isn't fair. But how the hell can I make them understand —I mean, it's fair to them—they're healthy, got jobs, lovers. I'm the one here in this fucking bed.

Looking down at my body makes me feel sad and tired. Five pounds of bone in a one-pound skin bag. Legs are invalid sticks. Sex a useless conduit for bloody waste. Arms bruised purple and yellow from IV's. This body, this stranger's body, hurts and puzzles me, and it's a sick feeling to think that I can't be the me I used to be. Not ever again.

And so this morning I ignore my breakfast, turn my face to the wall and leave it there until the dietitian is called.

We'd been friends, the dietitian and I, in happier days. She'd see I got sandwiches and Coke and snacks. Anything so long as I'd eat. But I got no friends now—no.

So she stands, half eager, half forlorn in a white uniform at the foot of my bed, dark hair scalloped Sassoon style around her earnest face, clutching a clipboard to her chest. "Willie," she says, "you didn't fill out any menus this week." She waits, looks at me. I wait, not looking at her. "So I just picked out a breakfast for you . . . I hope it's all right . . . Where should I put it? . . . Right here all right? . . . Let's see now, we've got fruit, ummm, grapefruit, and . . . Sugar Pops, and . . ."

"Mmmmble."

"Excuse me, what did you say?"

I stare right at her and, in deadly, clipped, I-am-speaking-to-a-foul-idiot tones, say "I . . . said . . . I . . . am . . . not . . . hungry." Then I stare at her as she leaves, and snap back into torpor.

I'm buying myself a big piece of solitude in which to brood. Because it's just not fair.

The Bells of New Canaan

Strange old Christmas Day.
Strange old Willie.

I've stopped fighting it. Whatever it is. I'm letting myself recover now, oh so slowly—they've got me up in a wheelchair now, three weeks after the operation.

But I feel tired and, well, somehow older. Slower. Quieter. I don't trust the process anymore, I don't trust in the future, don't believe anymore that everything's going to come out all right.

I don't *disbelieve* either. Somehow I feel if I just reserve judgment, if I don't *involve* myself quite so much with what's going on, with my progress, my health —if I don't fight so much, then I won't get hurt so hard, get dumped on my ass like with the bladder thing, with the visit home, with the fusion so long ago.

In the course of this wary nonattachment, I've gone to live deeper inside my skull—watching, waiting.

Strange old Willie.

Strange old Christmas Day.

An occasional flurry of wet snow from the gray skies mocked the notion of White Christmas—I didn't much give a shit, I hadn't been expecting much. The only time I started to get depressed was when my mother stopped by on the way to a Christmas party to give me my present. She couldn't stay long—Judy, too young for visiting privileges, was waiting in the car. But for the brief time she was there, I saw my Christmas through her eyes (poor kid) and was briefly brought down.

After she had gone, though, I bundled myself into the fancy bathrobe she'd given me, and trundled myself off to explore. Well, not so much to explore—I'd seen everything there was to see a dozen times—but to move around.

The setting was perfect for my mobile meditation; rolling thoughtfully down the empty halls with their sad fluorescent lighting, stopping by a gleaming hibernating machine in physical therapy, parking by the drained hydrotherapy tank, or nodding to the occasional nurse or aide who'd given up Christmas to have New Year's Day free, I began to enjoy a sort of muted melancholy.

Joan Kelly caught up to me by the weight racks in PT. "Willie," she said, "we need somebody to play guitar for the Christmas carols this afternoon. Can you help us out?"

Unnh. Christmas carols with the wasted ones. I flashed a quick picture of that one meal I'd had with them. Joan looked at me, I at her. "Sure. When?"

"About an hour. In the lounge."

Why the hell did I agree to do it? I asked myself, wheeling back to my room to roll a joint, take care of my head before the fest. Well, self, I answered, it's like, now that I'm not fighting it, I've got nothing more to fear from these people. Before I was terrified by their emptiness. Somehow, I'd thought, they've given it up, they quit fighting—and that was threatening to me. But now that I've been in that giving-up space myself, been in it and through it, it doesn't scare me anymore.

Sure, I'll play your fucking guitar. Soon as I finish this roach.

They're all waiting for me in the patients' lounge— crutches, canes, walkers, wheelchairs are strewn around the room, and there are, oh, about twenty old cripples gathered around the mock fireplace at the other end of the pastel-colored salmon and pink lounge. Some are in hospital gowns; others (like me) have changed or been changed into the nearest their limited hospital wardrobe can come to holiday finery. The men wear for the most part bright wool shirts that hang loosely on their frames. The women are in slacks—the better to hide urine bags, stumps, withered legs, what-have-you.

But their eyes, almost all of them, are brighter today, they're more alive than ever I've seen them. Why aren't they depressed, I ask myself, these old fucked-up cripples in a hospital on Christmas Day? But then I have to laugh. I'm a young fucked-up cripple in a hospital on Christmas Day. They're just like me, I think, we're all taking it one day at a time.

So deck them halls, hark them herald angels, and come upon a midnight clear. Luckily, Joan has a fake sheet for all the carols, so I just have to flatpick the chords and sing along with my wheezy wavery fellow warblers.

Then when we've done all the standards, when everyone's bathed in the rosy glow of good fellowship except for them that's lapsed into coma, I sing them the Stones' "No Expectations," sling my guitar behind my wheelchair, and head for my room, where I spend the rest of the day watching TV.

Good exit.

Steinman's Torture

The week after Christmas I was back in Physical Therapy working out—lifting weights, easing my way back to a standing position in the parallel bars, walking a few easy steps—when an aide informed me as follows: I was wanted in Steinman's office in an hour; in the meantime, I was to clip off my catheter, let the fluid build in my bladder. Here we go again. The next hour passed slowly.

Uh oh, I thought, as soon as I wheeled into Steinman's office, because he wasn't behind his desk. He was in the other room instead, in the torture room with the leather and steel obstetrics type table/chair that split in the middle, and had stirrups (the better to hold you with, my dear).

Double uh oh, because he had two other folks in the room with him, both white-clad, one a tall strong Puerto Rican aide from urology, the other his nurse.

"C'mon in, Willie," he said.

"Whoffo?" I asked suspiciously, but I wheeled in all the same. I guess I'd learned that all the bitching and struggling weren't going to save me an ounce of trouble. Go along with them, Willie, were my instructions to myself, do what you have to do, but reserve a private place inside your head. They can't touch that.

I parked beside the table. Steinman bent down, snipped the catheter, slipped it out, untied my leg bag. "Okay, son, up on the table. On your stomach."

On my stomach? Oh my ass, what now? The aide lifted me up, turned me over, adjusted me so my genitals hung through a cutout circle in the table.

"We should have an easier time getting you to void," Steinman said, "now that those bladder stones aren't fouling things up." I heard clicking and clacking as he busied himself arranging lethal-sounding instruments; face down on the table, I saw only cracked brown leather. "What we're going to do is called a pudendal block," he continued. "We're going to inject a fluid to deaden the nerve that controls the bladder sphincter."

"Far out. You just give me a shot in the ass and deaden one nerve?"

"Oh no. We're going to inject through the rectal wall and poke around to get that nerve. It will hurt a little."

Then I looked around, twisted my head to see something I wished I hadn't seen—a needle so long and wickedly thin it looked like a stage prop. Oh fuck. My stomach turned flippity flops, I tasted a bitter taste in the back of my throat. Then I pillowed my head on my already damp hands—I could smell the sweat—and fixed my mind on . . . okay . . . on what? . . . Got to have something to think about so's not to think about the needle . . . what do I know by heart? . . . *The Raven* . . . Onceuponamidnightdreary . . . I only knew the first stanza, up to rappingonmychamberdoor, so I repeated it top speed, screamed it inside, over and over, as the needle went in.

Strange thing. Pain started popping up all over—flashes of pain in my head, my neck, my throat, bladder, ass, head again. Flash pop flash—cold pain, till finally it was done.

They lifted me off the table, back into the wheelchair. I was feeling pretty blitzed out, but Jesus! at least I'd gotten through without breaking down. Felt like a victory.

"That was fine, thank you," Steinman told the nurse and aide. We left them to clean up and went into the bathroom. I transferred from the wheelchair to the toilet and pushed down hard on my bladder where he showed me. To my amazement, a thin trickle of piss splashed into the bowl. Only a trickle, and only for a few seconds, but the first I'd surrendered in a long time without the aide of a catheter.

It was like the good news/bad news jokes. The good news was that the procedure was working. The bad news was that it would have to be repeated several more times. "I'll see you Friday," Steinman said.

I went back to my room, rolled a joint, and sucked it like a baby sucks tit. It calmed me down a bit—my heart had been racing from the fear, the pain, the exertion—and I took the opportunity to look at that private space in my head. How did I feel about all this? Oh, a little sad that I was going to have to go through all that pain again. And a little tired. But not at all surprised. They couldn't surprise me anymore.

I Shall Be Free

Well, I guess the foregoing sort of gives you the tenor of the next couple of weeks of my life. I worked pretty hard—not as hard as I'd worked before the bladder operation, but steadily—and I got myself back into preoperation shape. I still jived with Lee and played cards with Joan, but I wasn't really relating to them. I most enjoyed getting back each afternoon to my empty room—they were keeping it empty, filling up other beds in the unit first, for which I was grateful. What I'd do back in my room was light up a joint (natch); watch Mike Douglas; have a tuna fish sandwich on soft white bread, a can of Coke, some codeine for dinner; watch the evening's TV; get a Seconal during the eleven o'clock news; and drift away during the "Tonight Show." Sometimes the night nurse would have to reach over my sleeping form and turn off the Late Late Show.

It would have been an idyllic existence—I'd resigned myself to the loneliness and boredom—but for the fact that twice a week, at eleven thirty in the morning, I'd hie myself to Dr. Steinman's office and face that rapierlike needle.

It was all worth it, though, when at last, after three weeks, I sat on that toilet and heard a thick stream of piss hit the water. I couldn't feel it, but I could hear it, and smell it, and, if I leaned over while pushing down on my bladder, see it. And boy that was good. It wasn't a giddy yahoo whoopee kind of feeling, like it might have been a few months ago, because I was still in that peculiar state of mind where I figured if I let myself get too brought up, I'm only gonna get further brought down at the next turn in the road.

But still, it felt *right*, it felt like a good thing to be able to do—to take a piss, even in this strange manual manner. It felt wonderfully lightening not to have to drag around a leg bag, wonderfully whole and healthy and manlike not to have that horrible rubber tube speared through my genitals.

So that day, in the third week of January, marked a quantum leap in my progress.

By the second week in February, I was gone, out of the hospital, without any dramatic good-byes, for I'd have to be back often for checkups.

On the ride back to the suburbs with my mother, I thought of that Dylan line where somebody asks him if it feels good to be free, and he asks back, "Are birds free from the chains of the skyway?"

17

My Day by Willie

One of the nurses at Farmington used to say, when I'd wish it were time for a shot, or wish I had a beer or something, "Be careful what you wish for, you just might get it." Then she'd cackle a witch's laugh.

Well oh my, Miss Dawson, truer words were never spoken. Because I've scarce been home a week and already I'm going out of my skull from boredom, feeling trapped and limited, feeling . . . yes, that's it—Christ, I feel like a shut-in. Remember those charity appeals to give books for shut-ins? And there were little articles in the newspaper about how cutting flowers out of paper and knitting tea cozies were great fun for shut-ins?

Yeah, sure. I could see how anything would look like fun compared to the way things are going lately. Oh, I know you don't want to hear me bitching anymore. And I don't mean to—I know inside that I'm much better off than I was before, and that the worst of this trapped feeling is only for a few days anyway, until the insurance money comes and I can get my car. Then everything'll be different. But for now . . .

I'm up around ten. My bladder won't let me sleep any longer. My legs hurt too, they're stiff, sore, sluggish. I snap on the back brace, use the wheelchair to get to the bathroom. There I'll sit, behind a closed door in the empty house (my mother's teaching, sister's at nursery school) for an hour, laboriously pushing piss out of a paralyzed bladder, pulling shit from a paralyzed colon.

It takes so long each morning just to get this poor fucked-up body going—it feels like each morning I have to get used to it again—it's heavy, sluggish, painful, and I can't help but remember this bathroom, summer mornings when I was a kid, and the delicious anticipatory feeling of a morning wash-up.

Now it hardly matters if I leave the bathroom. So by the time I've finished brushing my teeth—sitting down, drooling toothpaste on the chair, banging my chin on the sink—I've probably worked myself into a good-sized pity-party.

It'll take me twenty minutes to get dressed—I time it, and race myself each day. The leg braces are attached to the ugly black shoes—I cover them with Levi bells my mother bought me.

So I'm up, washed, dressed, my day awaits me. Now what? You tell me. I can make breakfast, wheel around the house, read the paper, read a book, watch TV, play guitar, play a record.

Or I can rise on my crutches and totter outside, mindful of each step. I can go out to the front yard, where I can watch the driveway and the front lawn. Or I can go to the back yard, where I can sit on the patio and watch the trees.

Yeah, there's lots of exciting things I can do. And

at three thirty, my mother comes home with Judy. A forty-six-year-old woman and a three-year-old girl. I don't even know what to say to them. I ask them about their respective school days, my mother and I have a cup of coffee, I make it somehow to dinner, and after dinner I watch TV or read until bedtime.

At night, Seconal-sleep. In my dreams I can always walk. I usually run.

It takes me longer to get out of bed with each successive morning.

Under the Golden Arches

This morning, though, is different. This morning is it! I whizz through my "toilet" as they say, doncha know, lahdedah, have a nervous cup of instant coffee, and sit in the living room, keeping an eye on the driveway through the big picture window. By ten thirty I've finished the paper, by eleven I've put it down, given up any pretence of reading. But by eleven thirty, there it is, crunching bluestone gravel in the driveway, beep! beep! A turquoise Impala.

I spring from my wheelchair, whoops, almost lose my balance, whoa now, settle myself into my crutches, head outside, down the short concrete walk to the car in the driveway. I open the door on the driver's side, the man in the gray mechanic's jumpsuit with the Chevy patch over the breast pocket slides over to the passenger's side, says, "It's all yours."

"Okay, let's go." He shows me how the hand controls work, and I spin my wheels in reverse, spewing gravel for yards. He checks me out on the controls, then we head for the Chevy place.

"Where from here?"

"Take a left at that next corner."

"Gotcha." I throw the wheel to the left, one-handing it by means of a suicide spinner knob, easing off on the gas with my left hand, pushing the hand control forward to tap the brakes, and the turquoise Impala corners screeching on two wheels, just missing the curb.

"Okay, joker," says the guy, "I think you got the idea of it." I drive him back to the showroom, around back to the service department, and let him off.

They wouldn't let me go without another half-hour's worth of instructions, caveats, advice.

"If anything goes wrong, bring it in, we'll fix it right away," said the service manager.

"Right," his assistant added. "We know how much you people depend on your cars."

Us people? Oh yeah, cripples. I'm in a new minority now.

Funny about this minority, though. I find when I'm sitting behind the wheel of this fresh set of wheels, smelling the Dee-troit new-car smell, I can pass—pass like a light-skinned spade, or a small-nosed blond Jew. I like the feeling. Too much.

On the way home from the Chevy shop, I decide to stop in at McDonald's. I've got it all figured out— I can hold the bag between my right hand and the crutch handle, and that way walk *and* transport my Big Mac to the car. Ah, the freedom to get a hamburger! How American!

But when I pull up to the golden arches, I am seized by an attack of stage fright. I've made such a beautiful entrance, with such élan, tires squealing, well-muscled left arm meaty out the window, and I picture myself as having made quite a hit. I project the picture of myself those little sixteen-year-old girls over in that Plymouth must have received, and then Cripple Willie takes over. My mind unreels the movie of me clambering awkwardly out of the car, fumbling with those shiny steel crutches, making way slowly, painfully, precariously, to the counter and back, and I play in my mind's projector an audience reaction shot— the girls' faces fading from admiration (with a suggestion of challenge) to pity.

Choke. I spin my wheels and flash off, hoping to leave the impression that the place just didn't have enough class for me. And I drive a mile down the road, to the Jack-in-the-Box drive-in, and order two tacos from the privacy of my front seat.

I didn't want a hamburger anyway. The girl at the window has light blue eyes in a dark tanned face, and they crinkle to laugh lines when she says thanks. I wonder if she can see the hand controls.

I park the car, and take a first big bite of the taco, and watch with dismay as the reddish brown tomatoey bean sauce squeezes out of the far end of the shell to fall plop! onto my shirt, drip onto my pants, and come to rest in a bloody, beany stain on the virgin vinyl of my front seat.

Fireside Chat

That evening found me sitting by the fire, doing that sort of idling-speed ruminating that our society condones only in front of fires and on toilets. All I wanted to do, really, was "stay in the moment" as they say, stay in the immediate present, because that felt pretty good—the soft rug, the firelight glancing off my father's dark walnut bookshelves. I wanted to stay in the present because thinking about the future gave me a jangled feeling inside like chewing aluminum foil.

It was simple shit that I didn't want to think about, like where was I going to live? If I just stayed here, lay back, let that fear grab me like today at McDonald's, shied away from being stared at, well then, I was going to turn into Cripple Willie for sure, for real. A cripple living home with a widowed mother—when the insurance money ran out I'd be going on welfare, making occasional forays out into the world, darting from psychic shadows in and out of normal people's vision, on the edge of sight where there are no colors, just black and white.

And at night I'd sneak into bed and hump my mattress while staring into the empty faces (yes the faces) of the girls in the tits'n'ass magazines.

Cripple Willie. I was scared to move and scared to stand still. So I just sat there on the rug in front of the fire. After awhile my mother came into the room with the sigh and the glass of Scotch and water that meant my sister was asleep and the day's work done.

Now, I'd had a strange relationship with my mother in the hospital, since the accident. Time is measured that way now—since the accident, before the accident. She'd been like a comforting object to me—a facile and useful object to be sure, able to talk and bring gifts and make me feel secure. But I didn't have to relate to her as a person, take into account *her* moods or needs, didn't have to give *her* any energy.

Didn't even have to talk to her if I didn't want to—sometimes she'd just sit there for an hour.

Nope, my mother was something that showed up at visiting hours and when I was in trouble. What there was in her that allowed her or enabled her or forced her to be that kind of compliant object for me then, I don't know, but that was how I'd gotten used to thinking of her.

So you can imagine how surprised I was when she sat down resolutely in my dead father's armchair, looked at her drink, and said what she had to say to me.

"First of all," she said, "you know you always have a home here with me. If that's what you want. But it's not. You don't want to live at home with me and be dependent on me. Now I don't know what you want to do about it, but I spoke to one of the deans out at State College, and he said they'd do everything they could to help you get started again out there." She paused, mumbled something I couldn't quite catch, repeated it. "You have an appointment to see him next Friday at three, if you want."

Inside I just started going off like fireworks. Cripple Willie yelled you can't do it, and another voice yelled how dare she make appointments for you, and another voice said thank God, you know you'd never have done it yourself. Part of me wanted to scream at her like a little boy in a tantrum—you know, just scream and turn red and pound my fists. But another part of the little boy wanted to hug her, say I love you mommy. Naturally, I kept a poker face, said, "You're right Ma. Thanks." Then we turned on the TV and watched Dean Martin insult his piano player.

18

Handicapped Driver

Though the car heater hissed with the slightly plastic breath that new car heaters always have, though it was a warm high fortyish February day—I shivered behind the wheel. No, not fever, just nerves, and my stomach was clenched tight because I was surely out there to sink or swim this time.

Except for that first abortive trip to McDonald's, except when I dragged myself to a movie—in a shopping center where I could park right in front of the entrance—I'd not been out in the world these two weeks home. But today, I have an appointment with the Dean of Undergraduates at State—I'd only seen the Dean once in the flesh during my entire freshman year, and then from the audience as he'd welcomed us to the university. But I was going to see him today, if it meant parking a mile away and dragging myself across uneven terrain and up stairs—I was going to have to carry this thing through or go home and hide under the bed with Cripple Willie.

Speaking of beds and Cripple Willie—god I was horny. That same day I'd gone to the movies, I'd stopped in at a stationery store. What the hell, I'd figured, it was only fifty steps away, might as well stock up.

You've gotta understand how *new* the world was to me, to my body; and me to the world, I'm sure. I was learning how to do everything again. Because my balance was fucked up—the hip muscles were paralyzed. and I couldn't feel my feet, they were way down below —it was like being on stilts.

So I had to figure out how to open the steel-rimmed glass door of the stationery store—how to throw enough weight against it without falling over. And I had to figure out how to keep my balance while reaching overhead (the crutch dangling from my forearm) for a magazine.

Here's where Cripple Willie comes in. You see, the mags I was reaching for were the men's mags, the male men's mammary type mags, and, you know, I was looking for something to take home with me. Because I'm twenty years old and I hadn't been laid in almost a year, and I was whacking off every night, and that's perfectly normal and average and it's okay, it's okay.

But Cripple Willie says, Ha, look at ya here, you can't even stand up, with those metal crutches and braces you look like a robot, you're pale and white and skinny and wasted, and you ain't never gonna get laid unless you wanna pay for it, and yucch, pity the poor whore—and on and on and on—thereby escalating the trivial act of buying a magazine into a full-blown crisis, leaving me shaken, my poor brain schizzed by a blizzard of paranoid mind chatter—*they* all *know* why you have to buy those mags, why you couldn't get laid

even if you tried and you're too scared even to try—
leaving me, as I say, shaken, at home, too depressed
even to jerk off.

When I turned past the gatehouse of State College,
I noticed the place sure hadn't changed much. New
parking lots, new buildings, still the same miasmal
muck of construction, mud, plank sidewalks. How the
fuck am I gonna get around here? I wondered. Be impossible if I was still in the wheelchair.

I scarcely have to tell you Cripple Willie was
screaming all sorts of dire oaths in my ear, but while
he was screaming, I was threading the car through
construction tunnels, narrow temporary driveways,
trying to drive as close as I could to the library building, where Administration was housed.

And then at last I came around one final turn,
to be greeted by the Deans' Parking Lot, a small asphalt
rectangle, with space enough for, oh, ten cars. The lot
was snuggled against the side of the library building
itself, and as I approached the space closest to the
library door serendipity struck, boom! flash!—an epiph-
any for me. It stood as high as a burning bush. It was
a metal sign. "Reserved for Handicapped Driver."

Handicapped Driver.

Me.

Handicapped Driver.

Me. I'd seen these signs all my life. Now, for the
first time, I *saw* one, and it was for me.

The sign, I don't know, *crystallized* things for me,
crystallized all Cripple Willie's rantings down to a
little cold hard place inside me that said—This Is It.

So I eased my turquoise Impala into the space, set
the hand brake, swung my braced legs out the door,

hauled my aluminum crutches out, and—clunk, clank
—tottered inside.

The visit with the Dean was anticlimactic. He gave
me keys to all the private elevators in all the buildings,
arranged for an unlimited parking sticker, preregistered
me for the next fall semester, gave me permission to
audit a few English courses *this* semester, wished me
luck, told me he admired my courage, told me to see
him if I needed anything else.

And this the Dean of Students! Man, I was in
like Flynn.

I used the Dean's secretary's phone to call the
number Capt Rico's mother had given me yesterday.
As long as I was out here, I reasoned . . .

Home Again, Home Again, Jiggity Jig

Tee-hee. I feel like I've been freed from a witch's
spell—I can hear her voice calling, but she has no *power*
over me—cackle away, you old bitch.

Just as a little test, I stopped off at a McDonald's
on the way out to Rico's. A couple of little kids stared
at me as I clattered in, one of them tugged his mother's
skirt, pointed, said, "That man has a broken leg."

Ha! Well, sure kid. Why not? This is what I was
afraid of? Somebody helped me carry my burger, fries
and Coke to the car, and that was that. On to Rico's.

I drove quietly through the dark winter afternoon,
taking lefts and rights and forks as Rico had directed,
and it seemed to me that with each mile the streets
grew wider, the lawns plusher, the houses larger, until
at last I turned down a gravel driveway shielded by a
colonnade of oak trees. I parked the car to the side and

slightly in front of the house, where a flagstone walk led to the front porch. As I unshipped my crutches from the back seat, I could hear the Stone's "Satisfaction" pounding from what must be one mother of a stereo system inside the house. It sure sounded like party time.

I stood up, tried my crutches on the gravel of the driveway, almost slipped, had to steady myself against the car. Tricky stuff. Then I started around to the walk, trying to be conscious of each step, of my weight, of my balance. In this fashion I made my way to the railed steps leading up to a front porch deserted save for a couple of tattered cats. At that point, almost home-free-all, I stopped, took a deep breath, and looked around.

Whew! Rico really had scored in the rent-a-home sweepstakes this semester. It was a huge two-story house with a porch running along almost the entire frontage; another porch outside the second floor windows; with a great lawn running at a slight downhill pitch some fifty yards to the road; with a thick sycamore tree set plump in the middle of the lawn, bare now, but with promise of lots of shade come spring.

I went up the steps, across the porch, and examined the two-door arrangement. There was a storm door that pulled open, and a big front door that pushed. I had to reason out a course of action—for a minute I wondered whether the rest of my life was going to seem like an improvisation upon an obstacle course.

Ah! I got it. Pull the storm door hard, interpose myself between it and the main door—boom! It closed by itself, slapping me in the rear. That's okay. I couldn't fall because I was wedged tight between the two doors.

I pushed the front door and propped it open with a crutch, then stepped inside as the storm door swung shut behind me. Then I closed the big door, which slammed shut with a final-sounding thud, and voilà! I was inside. In a living room with a half-dozen people, none of whom had noticed my entrance.

Well. If you've ever been a good solid hangin-out bum, beatnik, or hippie, if you've ever been to college in the last ten years or high school in the last five—you know the scene. A bunch of young people in various states of undress—some apparently just getting up for the day (at four in the afternoon), some getting up for the second or third time, some who've obviously been laid back down here in the living room all afternoon, listening to the loud stereo, smoking dope—all lounged around the living room floor, ignoring the middle-class furniture shoved out of the way along the periphery of the room.

At length a pretty girl with dark frizzy hair and gold-flecked eyes noticed me parked by the door. Her eyes narrowed, then widened. "Oh," she said, "you must be Willie. I'm Randi." Then she called over her shoulder, "Rico, he's here." At that everybody looked up at me, the record ended, and what with the sudden silence and the stares, I felt like I was at the center of a frozen vortex. Then Rico appeared across the room, and we stared at each other for a moment across the silence.

Quick moment. Theatrical. A lot passed between us, said by the eyes, left unsaid. Then I broke the silence—god how many times have I broken through potent silences with a wisecrack. "Nice store you got here, Mistah Ancis." A Lenny Bruce line. Rico finished off the bit, ". . . and two thousand tubes of airplane glue."

And that was about it. Home again.

Mu Tea

In the kitchen, alone, Rico and I almost said what we had to say. I sat at the round yellow table, rolling a joint from the wooden bowl of fixins set out; he puttered around the stove boiling up a pot of Mu tea.

"Mu tea!" I said. "You going organic on me, Capt?" He laughed behind his beard, began ferrying cups, honey, milk to the table.

"I don't know," he said, "I'm learning a lot from Randi. You want tea?"

"Yeah. You aaah . . . goin steady?"

"Better'n that. Shackin up!"

"Goin all the way?"

"Fuckin A." Well, there we were, jivin around again, but we couldn't sustain it, and the weight of the unsaid dragged us back down to a silence in which the rattle of the tea things echoed. I lit a joint and passed it across the table. He took a long toke, but instead of passing it back, he sat there looking at it. When he spoke he looked, not at me, but at the smoke floating up through the yellow room to the white ceiling. "I'm proud of you, man. A lot of times I wanted to tell you that, or just tell you I'd be around to help when you got out . . ."

"Hey . . ."

"Or just tell you I felt for you, tell you I knew how tough it must be, just see you through some of it." He passed the joint to me, took a short sip of the steaming dark tea. "But I couldn't. No, fuck that—I didn't. I don't know if you can forgive me for that . . ." He trailed off, and it was my turn to contemplate the room, and my friend, through the smoke.

"People have said that to me—visitors in the hospital, you know, or social workers," I told him. "They're proud of me, or how far I've come, or how much I've been through—and it's hard for me to relate to. I did what I did . . . just to get out of the hospital, I guess, and sometimes I just cried, you know? and didn't do anything, and I was scared and doped up a lot." With that obligatory disclaimer out of the way, I paused, passed the joint, stirred my tea. Then I looked over at Rico, he was looking back at me now, and I slapped the table so hard the cups rattled.

"But you know, goddammit, I did it! And for the rest of my fucking life, I'll know what I can do." I took the joint back from him and took an enormous toke, a championship toke, a Randle McMurphy Zorba the Greek toke. "I woke up paralyzed, man, and I built myself up—I learned how to dress myself, and stand, and walk, and . . . and . . . oh fuck—I did it. Whatever else happens, they can't take that away from me."

"Well then," said Rico, "we're both proud of you."

"Fuckin A!"

The shadows cast into the kitchen by the late afternoon sun lengthened, joined together, until it was dark, and we adjourned to the living room. The afternoon's loiterers had largely dispersed, leaving three of their number and a crackling fire. Rico and I joined the three ladies before the blaze.

215

"Willie," he said, "this is Miranda and Helen. You already know Randi."

"Hello girls," I said. Mmph. Did I catch some shit!

Miranda had dark skin, black hair cut short. She squinted her left eye, snarled at me out of the left side of her mouth, spitting consonants and hissing sibilants —I couldn't quite follow her. So Helen—pale-skinned, short brown hair, fleshy nose, brown eyes that had narrowed fiercely—explained in slower English, with firm leveling hand gestures, that I'd insulted them by calling them girls, that . . . and she went on, growing more excited, speaking louder, pitch rising, hands jerking spastically at face level—I mean she was really worked up.

And I was puzzled. Not because they didn't want to be called girls—social phenomena never involved me very much; I'd learned to call a black a black and would now know not to call a female a girl—but because they got so angry behind it. They were both spitting and slobbering away at me now; Randi was nodding in sisterhood (Rico just leaned back on his elbows and smiled—this was obviously not an isolated incident.)

Lemme tell you, I apologized like hell—I've always been good at recognizing superior forces (numerical and historical)—and in my best turneth-away-wrath wide-eyed softness asked them to hip me to what was going on. The fucking thing was, I realized—as the mollified women explained, argued, cajoled—I'd missed the whole beginning of the Women's Liberation Movement. Small wonder—I'd been in the closed world of the hospital for ten months, and the media were always at least six months behind what was *really* happening anyway.

But still, this was a reminder of how out of touch I might well be after nearly a year in the can, and I resolved to be more careful in the future.

Because in addition to being more just, more liberated, more conscious to be on the women's side—it was nice to have Helen over here next to me in front of the fire, with a nice soft tit just lightly brushing my arm.

With my faux pas forgiven, we settled down to a long chat and smoke. Rico told me how they'd sublet the house—it was a hundred and fifty years old—from an English professor. Helen had fronted for the gang with the prof, and she gave a fine demonstration of the crinkly face and papery whisper that had seduced the guy into renting his place to students while he was in Afghanistan taping primitives.

It was, at last, only hunger that moved us out of the cozy living room. Four of us, at Rico's suggestion, opted for Perelli's (best Italian food east of Mulberry Street)—Miranda passed. The others went upstairs to wash and change, while I lay on the living room carpet, before the fire, and scared myself with Cripple Willie visions of the night ahead. You know—simple shit like everybody walking ahead and me dragging my legs behind. Or me falling down at the entrance to the restaurant. Of course, the longer it took them to dress, the farther old C. W. carried things. By the time they reappeared at the top of the stairs, he had me and Helen—no, himself and Helen—in bed together, suffering eleven different kinds of embarrassing coital failure.

But when she smiled at me from the stairs—she

sure looked good in tight old jeans and a red blouse with flowing sleeves—it was like she turned down the volume on Cripple Willie; and as I struggled to my feet, headed for the front door, and opened it for my friends, the fears were transmuted to a simple case of stage fright. Even that disappeared when I was behind the wheel of the Impala, gunning the engine.

Climax

A big oak tree towered ahead of us, dead ahead of us, and both women—Helen in front with me, Randi in back with Rico—sucked in air with a "hunh" of surprise. Rico just laughed because he knew I knew the road, and in fact I'd already tapped the brakes once, twice, and started the power slide that would take us around the sharp left in front of the tree.

"Willie," said Helen, "please slow down," and something in her voice went right through me—she was scared. A year ago I'd have laughed at her, but I knew more about being scared now, and I slowed down to the speed limit.

"Don't worry," I told her, "I'm a good driver. I never had a ticket or an accident."

"That don't mean you're a good driver," Rico put in from the back. "Good drivers have tickets and accidents like good knife fighters have scars." Well, maybe. We'd discussed that before. I'd've been inclined to agree with him, but for Helen's sake, I kept to a reasonable rate of speed. It felt good being concerned about someone else's state of mind. For once. Lord, I must have been a petty tyrant in the hospital, where my self-centeredness was encouraged.

So we took it easy on the back roads, heading east,

and I rather enjoyed gliding the car easily through the scrubby woodland. A couple of joints were being passed around the car, and we were discussing the theme Rico had presented earlier. "Good lovers get clap and pregnant," suggested Helen. "Good dealers get busted," said Randi. And so on, stoned and happy and close until the red and green lights of Perelli's, strung on wires like a used-car lot, appeared around a last curve.

I guess it was just about in the middle of my linguine and red clam sauce that I recognized that happy warm feeling inside me. It was like being home again, and all those fears of being a cripple living forever with Mama were nowhere now. Just being in Perelli's again, with friends and a girl, was really all I'd wanted when I'd wanted out of the hospital so bad. And . . .

Here I was. It made the rest of the evening slightly anticlimactic, or . . . no, not anticlimactic, but a long slow climax, prolonged enough to recognize and hold, and savor—all of it: from the meal and the chatter and the dessert to the realization that some kind of real contact was happening between Helen and me; through the long ride home, and the long, agonizingly long cup of tea and conversation in the kitchen of Rico's old house.

It was just two people trying to get to know each other before bed—that's why we talked till after midnight. But, you know, I sometimes think if I had back all the time I spent in conversation, light or heavy, with girls, as nights grew old, older, ancient, when all I really wanted to say was, let's fuck—I think if I had those times back, I'd only be about twelve years old today.

But we made it upstairs to Helen's bedroom, kissed

once, and then she smiled and went off to the bathroom. I guess I was grateful for the opportunity to fumble off my back and leg braces in privacy.

What can I tell you? We made it? It was good? I could do it? Yeah, all of those.

And waking up the next morning, lying there quietly watching Helen sleep, while the sun poured in through the bedroom window—that was the icing on the cake. Sweet. It was sweet.

I stayed over Saturday too—so I skip my pills for one day—it won't kill me—and only went home Sunday night because I had on Monday a couple of appointments I couldn't miss.

After all, I had the future to get ready for.

I'm a Vipple

Two appointments today—one here at VIP, one with Dr. Hassel at Ryder—but I feel like I could handle two hundred.

VIP—that's Vocational Improvement Program. Federal money, the Dean had told me when he made the appointment for me, administered by the state, and they're obliged to assist any legitimately handicapped person (that's me) with his vocational needs (that's college). I figured for sure they'd have some parking spaces set aside for the handicapped, but I cruised the lot twice with no luck. Then I pulled into a space marked "Director," wrote a note that said "Handicapped Driver" and stuck it in my windshield wiper. Let em try and tow me.

I felt cocky all the way up the elevator to the waiting room, but I was not ready for what awaited me there. Looked like the cast auditions for a musical version of Todd Browning's Freaks. People were wheeling, dragging, throwing their twisted bodies in and out—whoops, there goes a quadruple amputee crawling in on his belly, application in his teeth.

Just kidding. But not by much. There was a severely retarded CP sitting across from me with his mother. He kept trying to talk to me, only I couldn't understand a word but neither could I ignore him, with his mother right there. So he went blagga blagga, and I smiled (my face hurt from smiling) and said what? and he said blagga blagga blagga. I felt guilty that I couldn't understand him. Maybe if I just went blagga blagga back? Naah, his mother would've killed me.

Compared to the waiting room, the interview was a snap. I figured I had the whole scene covered.

Yes ma'am, well I hope someday to be a writer, but I recognize that that takes awhile, so I'll start by studying English, with an eye toward getting a teaching certificate to tide me over.

Outasite, kid, you're covered for tuition, fees, and books—more when the insurance money runs out, just a pro forma examination by our consulting physiatrist next week. See me during the midsemester break. Bye now. Miss Press, send in that family of microcephalics —the cute ones with the matching dresses.

Goin to college. Rah. Rah. Rah.

Why the scene in the waiting room didn't upset me I don't know—maybe I was still feeling strong and good from the weekend. Maybe I would feel strong and good from now on. Could be.

But I was feeling pretty good about myself and my

uh handicap—didja see the way I handled that parking space?—and I still had one more appointment, in the city, to get some school medical forms filled out by Dr. Hassel.

The Impala took to the Expressway like an old lover, and I drove west to New Canaan Hospital.

No Sympathy for the Devil

It was amazing, just amazing, now the distance between the circular entrance to Ryder and the doorway had shrunk, and I really had to wrench my mind back to remember those first prideful tottering steps to my mother's waiting car, that first furlough weekend.

Inside, the same gang was there (and why not, for them it had been a few months of business as usual since my last checkup) and they all seemed glad to see me. After seeing Hassel, I joined Lee and some others in the PT's room, we strewed ourselves casually about the narrow room, pushing aside piles of paper to sit on desks, on arms of chairs. They caught me up on hospital gossip, not much, and then asked—what else?—how things were going with me.

"I'm doing fine," I said. "Far out. Gonna go to college, start next semester. I can walk as far as I have to, don't hardly use the wheelchair, bladder's fine."

"That's fantastic, Willie," somebody said. "We're all very proud of you."

"Yeah, proud," they echoed. "Prize patient . . . doing fine."

Jesus fuck, I thought, we have nothing to say to each other, even Lee and me.

"How's Dr. Woodson?" I asked.

"He's doing fine too. Teaching neurology out in Ohio. Using the full crutches and braces, walking more than we thought he would."

"Oh yeah, we're proud of both of you . . . prize patients."

Then Lee leaned over to me. The others followed him with their eyes, stilled their chatter, let him speak. "Look, Willie, it's fantastic luck you came by today. Would you do us a favor?"

"Sure, um, what?"

"We got a girl paraplegic in a few days ago. They transferred her over from Rusk—she wouldn't work, you know how they feel about *that*, and we haven't been able to do a thing with her. A real solid posttrauma depression, eats a little, won't drink, won't work."

"What do you want me to do?" I asked, with a sinking feeling, knowing full well what they wanted me to do.

"Well, we thought, I mean, she's your age and all, same level of injury, you could go in, just talk to her."

"A pep talk, man! I can't do that."

"So just go in, she's in your old room, say you're visiting for old time's sake, talk to her, at least she'll see what's possible."

"It won't work, man. These crutches only look good to us cause we know where I came from, what the choices were. They're gonna look like shit to her."

"Just try it, Willie," Lee asked. "Try it," the PT's chorused. "For me," said Lee. "For us," they said.

"My old room?"

"Yeah, thanks. I knew you wouldn't let us down."

Walking down the corridor that connects the therapy wing and the inpatient, thinking of the first walk Dr. Woodson and I took, the sweat and the feeling of triumph, trying to think of what I'd say to this girl— I felt sick. Only a noncripple would send a cripple to cheer up a cripple. Don't they know, I thought, that when we're depressed, we depress each other.

I got a hello and a peck on the cheek from Nurse O'Hara, and it took me decades to walk the last twenty yards to my room. I paused outside, feeling my breath rasping in the top of my lungs, breathing shallow, fast. What the fuck am I so scared about? What am I going to look like to her?

I took a deep breath, looked in, to the left, at Dr. Woodson's bed, empty now, then to the right, to my bed.

In it lay a sad, skinny little girl. Click. Click. My eyes took in the cloudy urine bottle, the tube running from the bottle to disappear under the sheets (into her cunt, I knew, crusty and unfelt). I saw her thin arms, splotched purple from IV's, the spurned water pitcher at the bedside. I saw her lank dull hair, heard the TV prattling away—ding ding, that's Double Jeopardy, Mrs. Pfeifer—and then, when she turned her gaze from the TV, to me in the doorway, I saw the depths of my own blackest moments reflected in the dull brown eyes.

Oh God, I thought. Baby, baby. I know. I know.

"Sorry," I said, "wrong room." And left Ryder by a side corridor, leading away from the therapy room. I circled around to my car, and left rubber in a squealing exit from the drive. I haven't been back, except once, last year, to remember for this book, but everyone I'd known was gone.

San Francisco, July 1974

	DATE DUE